*Spare-Time Businesses
You Can Start and Run
with Less Than $1,500*

Other Books by the Author:

*How to Make Big Money at Home
    in Your Spare Time*

How to Make Big Profits in Service Businesses

Second Income Money Makers

How Self-Made Millionaires Build Their Fortunes

Spare-Time Businesses You Can Start and Run with Less Than $1,500

Scott Witt

Parker Publishing Company, Inc.

West Nyack, New York

© 1980, *by*

PARKER PUBLISHING COMPANY, INC.

West Nyack, N.Y.

Library of Congress Cataloging in Publication Data

Witt, Scott.
   Spare-time businesses you can start and run
with less than $1,500.

   Includes index.
   1. Success. 2. Business. 3. Self-employed.
I. Title.
HF5386.W643   658.1'141   79-18074
ISBN 0-13-824169-4

Printed in the United States of America

What This Book Will Do for You

How would you like to start with $1,300 and become a millionaire? Or put $650 into a spare-time business that pays you back at the rate of $2,000 per week? This books tells how it has been done and how it can still be done.

You may wonder how I can be so sure that this kind of success is achievable. I know because I have seen people do it; not just one time but in many instances where people start from scratch and build fortunes for themselves.

"Yes," you say, "but they must be geniuses."

Perhaps a few of them are. But let me tell you something that I have learned throughout my career as a wealth educator. Most people who have built fortunes for themselves are very much like you and me, people with everyday abilities who discovered that there is a big market for those abilities, provided they are applied in the right manner. And that's what this book is all about. It shows how to take one or more of your own "everyday" abilities and use it to build a fortune.

In doing so, you have an advantage that many others have not had. You have this book as your guide. The fortune-building methods explained in these pages are based on my exhaustive research into the success techniques of people who have already achieved their wealth goals.

THE KEY TO INSTANT WEALTH SUCCESS

It doesn't take a lot of skill or knowledge to become rich. The case histories throughout this book prove that. It certainly doesn't take a big investment. Any of the hundreds of money-making plans you are about to learn of can be started with an out-of-pocket investment of less than $1,500. And it doesn't take too much of your time. All of the ventures outlined here can be run "after hours," which allows you to continue in your full-time occupation until you feel like quitting.

The key to instant wealth success, then, is not outstanding skill, a big investment, or time. The key is to take an ordinary skill and then do something extraordinary with it. You apply that skill to create a product or service that people need badly and for which they are willing to pay you well.

HUNDREDS OF BUSINESS PLANS TO CHOOSE FROM

When I say you can find wealth success by reading this book, it's partly because of the wide variety of high-potential business opportunities I've assembled here for you. Can you make things with your hands? Then you'll want to latch on to one of the proven money-makers in Chapter 2, which deals with producing profitable products at home.

Perhaps you're handy at fixing things. Most repairmen don't know how to make a lot of money, but Chapter 3 tells how you can be a notable exception to the rule.

You may like working with gadgets or machines. Did you know that there are scores of gadgets and machines that can make a mint for you? They're explained right here.

Dealing successfully with others is a skill possessed by a lot of people. If you're one of them, there are ways to apply that skill so that other people will actually build a fortune for you. I'll tell you how.

You may be intrigued by the money that others are making in mail order. Perhaps you've even tried your hand at it. Chapter 6 reveals why most people don't make fortunes in mail order, how a select few do, and how you can guarantee your own success in this fascinating field.

Do you like telling others what to do? Big money awaits you if you cash in on the seminar and training boom, as explained in these pages.

Or perhaps you enjoy writing, photography, or art. Thanks to my years of research, you'll learn how certain craftsmen in these fields make the really big money, while those who don't know "the secret" slave away with little to show for their efforts.

How about cash investments? Would you like to learn how to take less than $1,500 and convert it into a fortune worth hundreds of thousands or even millions of dollars? It's been done many times, thanks to the techniques you'll learn in Chapter 12.

A COMPLETE WEALTH-BUILDING PROGRAM

Please don't be mistaken. This book isn't like so many others that merely list business "ideas." It goes into detail—step-by-step detail—on how to get your money-maker rolling and how to build it to the fortune-producing level you desire. These instructions have been carefully compiled on the basis of what other people have already done and are doing now.

What they are doing, you can do—sooner than you may think.

Scott Witt

Contents

1

How to Make Big Money Starting with Very Little Cash

The best way to make a lot of money in your spare time is to work for yourself. Labor for somebody else and you may make three, four, or five dollars an hour—and perhaps get laid off if the boss decides he dislikes you. Work for yourself and you call the shots—and by picking the right business you can earn $20, $50, or even several hundred dollars an hour.

WHY IT DOESN'T TAKE A LOT TO MAKE A LOT

Many people hesitate to start their own spare-time businesses because they think a big investment is required. It's just not so. The fact is, there are thousands of people happily running their own spare-time businesses today, earning hundreds or even thousands of dollars a week, after starting with investments of under $1,500. This book is about such people. It tells how they did it, and how you can do it, too.

How can you make really big money starting with a tiny investment? By doing as these people did:

- Pick a business that requires very little outlay for inventory or equipment.

- Work out of your home instead of renting an office or shop.
- Choose an enterprise that utilizes skills or experience you already have.
- Learn how to have your customers foot the bills right from the start.
- Offer a product or service that costs little to produce, but brings top dollar in the marketplace.

These are just a few of the techniques you'll have at your command as you progress through this book. You'll see how others have done it and you'll learn, step by step, how you can repeat their success, building a giant money-maker for yourself in your spare time.

As a starter, let's pick just one of the many thousands of case histories from my files on personal business success. We'll see how each of the above techniques was employed by a man who began with $1,200 a few years ago and has built a thriving business.

LITTLE OUTLAY FOR INVENTORY OR EQUIPMENT

Frank T. had a regular job as an appliance salesman. He had also worked spare time as a bartender, but realized that there must be a better way to earn money during the hours he was free from his regular job. He found that way by starting a mail order business dealing in "special interest" books. The "special interest" was customized vans—a longtime hobby of his that is shared by hundreds of thousands of Americans who buy van-type vehicles and then customize them according to their individual tastes.

The only pieces of equipment required to start Frank's mail order business were a typewriter and a postage scale. He already owned the typewriter, and he bought the scale.

The inventory consisted of his starting supply of books, which as you'll see presently, cost him a fraction of their retail worth.

The rest of his start-up budget went toward reproducing a small catalog listing his books on the subject of customized vans, and placing some small classified ads in a number of national magazines.

Here's what the start-up costs came to:

Postage scale	$ 45.00
Inventory	700.00
Catalog flyers	200.00
Classified ads	205.00
Incidental expenses	50.00

The incidental expenses included a business registration fee, postage for mailing out the initial orders, some stationery, and a loose-leaf book in which he kept his records.

NO RENTAL EXPENSE

One of the biggest expenses for most new businesses is leasing a store, office, or shop. Frank avoided this cost entirely by using part of his recreation room as his office and warehouse.

"The books are kept in cartons next to the work table that I use for packing the orders. At a right angle to that table I have a desk and my typewriter. The whole thing takes up only one third of the space in the room, leaving a large area for the 'recreation' part of my rec room," Frank explains. He adds, "Most of my recreation, though, comes from the business part of the room. For pure enjoyment, nothing in my life has equaled the pleasure of running this business and watching it grow and prosper."

UTILIZING SKILLS AND EXPERIENCE

Why did Frank choose books on customized vans as his mail order specialty? "Because vans had been a longtime hobby of mine," he reports. "I'd read just about every book and magazine on the subject, so I knew what was available and just what other people would want to read—especially the people whose interest in vans was a recent one.

"Whenever someone takes up a new hobby, he or she naturally wants to learn as much about it as possible—and as soon as possible. Such people are prime prospects for the sale of books and publications dealing with their new interest."

Frank's involvement with vans and his knowledge of the subject clearly worked to his favor when he started his book business.

CUSTOMERS FOOT THE BILLS

Frank's business is run on a cash-with-order basis. Since his books sell for four or five times what he pays for them, the money received in today's mail more than pays for tomorrow's supply.

Here's how it works. The average order that Frank receives amounts to $13.50 (most customers buy more than one book). Of this, 25% accounts for the wholesale cost of the books and the expense of having them shipped to his home. About 7½% pays for shipping and handling the volumes that leave his home, 33% goes for advertising, and 33% covers his incidental expenses and profit.

Let's look at what happens to the $13.50 received in a typical order:

Money received	$13.50
Cost of books	3.38
Handling & shipping	1.00
Advertising	4.56
Incidental expenses	1.86
Profit	2.70

It's easy to see that cash is readily available to replace the books that are sold. The $3.38 deducted from the typical $13.50 order takes care of that. And to allow his business to grow, Frank often takes some cash from his profit allotment to enlarge his inventory. Thus, in a given month, he may take 15% as profit and put 5% into expanding his inventory.

LOW-COST PRODUCT, TOP-DOLLAR INCOME

You may wonder how Frank is able to purchase books for one fourth of their retail value, paying 25% instead of the 60% or more that most book dealers have to pay. The answer is that Frank deals in publishers' overstocks. These are books that the publisher has stopped printing. The remaining supply is then sold to a wholesale firm that deals in "overstocks" or "remainders." The wholesaler buys them for a small fraction of their original cost, adds on his profit, and sells them to individual dealers at far below what the cost would have been when the volumes were first published.

"I can sell books that are several years old," Frank explains, "because people who are just becoming interested in vans are anxious to get all the 'know-how' on customizing that they can. Most bookstores don't handle these books—or if they do, they just have one or two titles in stock. I have dozens. So the van enthusiasts turn to people like me to get their information. And they're happy to pay the full retail price, especially since they couldn't find the books they need anywhere else."

Working only about two hours a day, Frank is already clearing about $300 each week in his business. And having achieved success with books in the van field, he's now planning to expand into a new line of books.

"There are a lot of overstock books out there waiting to be sold to people with special interests," he states, "and I'm ready to be the man who supplies these books to them."

What's the new field he's thinking of? "That's a business secret," Frank replies.

YOUR MOST VALUABLE ASSET—YOUR SPARE TIME

Your choice of a spare-time money-making project may not be anything like Frank's. Van conversions probably aren't your field at all, selling books may not interest you, and you may prefer something other than mail order. But no matter what your interest, and regardless of your experience and skills, you'll find a venture in this book that can make your spare time the most valuable part of your day.

How do I know? For one thing, there are so many business plans presented in the next 12 chapters that at least one and perhaps several must be right down your alley.

And even more important, each of these ventures has been proven successful by people who are reaping big incomes from them at this very moment. As a business consultant, writer, and commentator, I have had personal contact with many of the people you'll be meeting. They've allowed me to study their enterprises inside out. Having spent the better part of my adult working life in this pursuit, I've been able to determine the precise methods that spell success for the part-time entrepreneur.

These methods are fully explained in this book, with emphasis on the shortcuts that will speed up your business success. Thanks to the detailed tips contained here, you should be able to avoid most of the pitfalls that have slowed the progress of many beginning wealth-builders. In other words, you'll be guided to make the right moves in starting and running your business, and you'll be detoured past the mistakes that befall many newcomers.

MAKE MORE AND KEEP MORE

There's one distinct advantage that you'll gain almost immediately as you start out in your part-time venture. You'll get to keep more of the money you make. This includes not only the money earned in your business, but also any other income you may have whether it is from a regular job or from other investments.

This is because employees and those who make standard investments don't benefit from the tax advantages that are open only to businesspeople. Once you go into business for yourself, you can start taking deductions that were not available to you before. These deductions are for such business-related expenses as:

- Association dues
- Books and magazines
- Employees' salaries
- Entertainment
- Equipment
- Insurance
- Lodging away from home
- Payments to a retirement plan
- Rent or amortization
- Training
- Travel
- Utilities

This is far from a complete list of deductions you may take as a person in business. In fact, it includes only items that can benefit you personally as well as in business. Allow me to explain.

SAVE ON PERSONAL EXPENSES

The government permits you to deduct any legitimate business expense. It is not generally concerned about the wisdom of making those expenses; all it usually cares about is whether or not they were incurred for the business. If such business expenditures also happen to benefit you personally, that's better still.

To get an idea of how you can benefit from this, let's look at the experience of a California widow, Martha L., who runs a bookkeeping service from her home. Martha keeps the books and sends out bills for many business and professional people in her town—mostly people whose businesses or practices are not large enough to warrant the hiring of an "in-house" bookkeeper.

As her business began to grow, Martha found that she had less and less time to keep up her home and property. She enjoyed housekeeping and maintaining her lawn and garden, but the business was cutting into the time available for this.

She thought of hiring a part-timer or two to help her with these chores. But then, smart businesswoman that she is, she thought better of it. Under her circumstances, the salaries of household helpers are not normally deductible. But the salaries of people who work for one's business are definitely deductible.

So Martha decided to hire a bookkeeper to work in her business. The salary is a legitimate business expense, and the work performed by the employee frees Martha to do the gardening and housekeeping that she enjoys so much.

"I look at it this way," Martha says. "I'm saving about one third of my employee's pay. If I'd hired someone to help out around the house, no deduction would have been possible. By switching the work assignment to the business instead of the house, the payroll is deducted from the amount of profit I must report to the government, and that adds up to quite a lot of saved tax dollars."

ENRICH YOUR PERSONAL LIFE

Martha has gained many other tax advantages from her bookkeeping business. Seeing what she did will help you in your own enterprise. Here are some examples:

- *Books and Magazines.* Many business-related books that Martha would be buying anyway can now be listed as deductions from her business profits.
- *Equipment.* Martha's teenaged son is an electronics hobbyist. When he became interested in home computers, she bought one for him to use in his spare time. The rest of the time it is busy handling many of her business chores—and is therefore a deductible item.
- *Insurance.* Since her business is operated in her home, part of the cost of insuring the home is listed as a business expense.
- *Lodging.* When Martha travels to her conventions, her hotel bills are naturally paid by the business, which means that the government is sharing the cost, thanks to the tax-deductible nature of this expense.
- *Retirement Payments.* Martha has set up a Keogh retirement plan, which allows her to defer paying taxes on the first $7500 of her net income. This is money that is set aside for her retire-

ment. No taxes will have to be paid on it—or on the interest it earns—until she retires. "And at that time," she explains, "I'll be in a lower income bracket, so the taxes will be lower."

- *Training.* Since Martha's son maintains their computer system, the cost of several electronics courses he took has been deducted as a business expense. Never mind the fact that he would have taken these courses anyway—they are now considered a requirement of the business.

- *Travel.* Martha likes to see as much of the country as she can, and she makes a point of attending the annual conventions of several professional groups to which she belongs. The travel is, of course, tax deductible.

- *Utilities.* Electricity and heat are expenses incurred in every household, but in Martha's home part of the cost is borne by her business, and thus is deducted from the gross profit figures.

PUT YOUR SPARE TIME TO WORK FOR YOU

Thanks to the tax advantages, you not only work in a spare-time business, but the business actually works for you. Even before you count your income, it can provide many benefits you might not otherwise be able to enjoy.

And when you do count your income, that's when the benefits really begin to pile up. People who operate part-time businesses such as the ventures to be outlined in this book find themselves in the position of not only earning a lot of money—but having the time to enjoy it as well.

Working a relatively few hours per week, you have both the time and the cash to pursue your personal interests and hobbies. Many of the business plans you'll be learning about allow you to set your own hours. You can adjust your work schedule to find time for extended vacations, travel, skiing, sailing, lazing about the house, or doing whatever you'd like to do.

That's the wonderful thing about a spare-time business. It doesn't have to hold you down. Unlike a store in a shopping center that must be opened every business day for the entire day, you can usually schedule your working hours to fit your own needs.

USE EVERYDAY SKILLS TO BUILD A PERSONAL FORTUNE

This chapter began by noting that it doesn't take a lot to make a lot. We were speaking then of money requirements. Now we're talking about required skills and knowledge. Once again, it doesn't take a lot to make a lot. You don't need outstanding skill or great knowledge to make a lot of money in your spare time.

I'd like to let you in on a little secret:

You already have the basic skills required for building a personal fortune in your spare time.

I know this for a fact, without even knowing you or your background. I know it because *everyone* has the basic skills required to operate a successful and highly profitable business. Then why isn't everyone making an awful lot of money in his or her own business? Because most people haven't discovered how to apply those skills. And that, my friend, is the purpose of this book.

Together, we're going to examine your own background and compare it with easily-run businesses that closely match your abilities. You'll discover, as you progress through the book, that there are dozens of businesses you could easily handle. You'll learn how to pick the one business that you will actually launch, based on the present customer demand for the product or service it features.

Thanks to the hundreds of business opportunities I've assembled here, you'll have no trouble matching up your abilities with a proven money-making plan.

Does that mean that you'll need absolutely no training at all? It depends. Here are two of the prime factors to consider when choosing a business:

1. Your ability to conduct the business
2. The saleability of its product or service

When you find a plan in this book that meets both criteria, you have a winner going for you. You might discover an even greater business opportunity that requires a skill that you have not yet developed. If the money-making potential is sufficiently large, then it might pay to obtain the added training that is required. And it can be a lot easier than you might think.

In the course of the book, you'll be shown various ways to get any training you might need, along with examples of how others have done it. But please follow this rule:

You should first consider the businesses that match abilities you already have. Only when you discover a far greater opportunity should you think of acquiring new skills.

Rest assured that you will find many opportunities here that do indeed match your everyday skills. It's important to remember that, mundane as these skills might appear to you, you do have a unique background. You will be able to profit from your:

- Friendships
- Hobbies
- Natural talents
- Personal reading
- Schooling
- Special interests
- Travels
- Work experience

Since no two people are exactly alike, each person (including you) has a unique blend of experience, skills, personal associations, interests, and personal background. That's why this book contains 11 different spare-time business categories, with a chapter devoted to each. And within each category there are dozens of variations listed for you to choose from.

Thus, if mail order is the field you choose, you'll find a compilation of 50 proven mail order sellers—items you can begin to sell right away for an immediate profit and rapid growth.

If your choice is handcrafting items at home, you'll be shown how to go about it—along with ideas for scores of home-produced items that are badly wanted by the public.

On the other hand, you may decide to profit from this age of mechanization. Chapter 4 is entirely devoted to machines—and how to pick one that can build a personal fortune for you.

A careful examination of the Table of Contents will familiarize you with the many opportunities available. The point is that so many opportunities are offered in so many fields that you'll find yourself saying, "Why, I could do that!" as you encounter the step-by-step plans.

INSTANT BUSINESS KNOWLEDGE

In order for this book to do the most for you, there is one thing you must do. And that is to read all of the chapters, whether or not the category is of particular interest to you. I give this advice for several reasons:

1. Although you may not be interested in conducting a repair and maintenance business, for example, there is a lot of valuable information contained in Chapter 3 that will help you in conducting whatever type of business you choose.

2. You may be pleasantly surprised to find that a category that does not appeal to you at first glance "grows on you" as you read about it and learn how other people like you have succeeded in it.

3. A thorough reading of all the chapters can serve as a valuable business education. The information compiled here stems from the experience of thousands of highly successful spare-time entrepreneurs. When I tell you that a certain business plan has proven to be profitable, I mean that many different individuals in many different locales have profited from it. What they have learned and what they have done can be the basis of your business education.

4. Although I don't expect that you will remember every technique, tip, and bit of data contained in these pages, you will be able, after reading the book straight through, to recall where such information can be found. For example, if you choose a plan contained in Chapter 12, you may recall that there was some information in Chapters 3, 5, and 10 that could be particularly helpful to you.

5. By the time you reach Chapter 13, you'll know enough about how to conduct a profitable spare-time business that you'll find the 21 shorter business plans presented there easy to understand and launch. These plans are in the final chapter because they don't fit into any of the chapter categories preceding them. Thanks to all the knowledge you've gained from the earlier chapters, the information in Chapter 13 is enough to put you on the road to excellent spare-time profits.

START A BUSINESS IN YOUR OWN HOME OR APARTMENT

An important advantage of a spare-time business is that it is also a "spare-space" business. The businesses described in the forthcoming chapters are designed not only to fit into whatever spare-time hours you have available, but they also fit into whatever spare space you have available.

Whatever your business requires, whether it's an office, shop, factory, studio, or production center, will fit into the space you have available. That's because one of the criteria involved in choosing your business will be space availability.

Once again, there is such a large selection of businesses to choose from that you'll have no trouble finding one to fit. These businesses can be conducted from:

- A corner desk or table
- Back yard
- Basement workshop
- Den
- Garage
- Kitchen table
- Living room
- Recreation room
- Spare room

You may wonder about the listing of a corner desk or table. Yes, there are a number of plans that require no more space than that. Such money-making plans can often be conducted entirely through the mail or on the telephone. One of the most profitable business plans, in which I have personally been engaged, required just a desk and a file folder, and it is presented in this book.

Although your home or apartment will probably serve as your "headquarters" there is no need for your business to keep you confined there. A number of the plans in this book will have you out in the community, meeting needs that will prompt people to pay you "top dollar."

LOOK TO THE FUTURE AND FULL-TIME WEALTH-BUILDING

Spare-time now and full-time later? That's the goal of many novice businesspeople. A business that is launched from your home on a part-time basis can become so profitable that it makes sense to quit your regular job and devote full time to the continued growth of your own enterprise.

It made sense to Harrison G., whose home served as the head-quarters of a growing flea market enterprise. Harrison's operation consisted of renting halls and ball fields where he conducted antiques flea markets in his area. The "book work" was done at home in the evenings and the flea markets were conducted on weekends.

"But as the number of booth rentals grew," Harrison recalls, "so did the preparatory work. Naturally, my profits were increasing as well. I realized that by leaving my regular job, I could allow my business to grow to its full potential. And I'm glad I made the decision. I'm now earning three times what I used to make on the job and in the part-time business."

You don't have to make the decision about going full-time until well after your business is established and prospering. But it's nice to know that the possibility exists.

THE ADVANTAGES OF PART-TIME NOW, FULL-TIME LATER

You have a lot going for you when you start a money-making program part-time with limited capital:

- You risk only your time and relatively few dollars
- Your regular source of income can continue to support you during the start-up days of your business
- If you don't need the business profits to augment your income, you can use them to expand the business
- If, as occasionally happens, you decide you don't like the type of business you've started, it's easy to switch to another enterprise
- Depending on the type of business, you may be able to operate several wealth-building programs simultaneously
- When the profits begin to equal your "regular" income you can think seriously about quitting your job and going full-time

People who start out in business on a full-time basis don't have these advantages. It's clear that as a part-timer, you'll have many more options open to you.

"OPTIONIZE" YOUR OPPORTUNITIES

"I call it optionizing," says wealth-builder Paul M. "I had enough money saved from my work as an advertising agency account executive to go into business full-time. But I knew that in my case it would not be wise."

Paul had examined a number of business opportunities and was pleased to discover that the ones he liked the most could be started and operated while he held on to his career job.

"My first business was to start a local advertising agency of my own. I prepared newspaper ads for local businesses. I did the writing and the layout work on evenings and weekends. It didn't conflict with my regular job because I worked for a major advertising agency that handled only national accounts."

As the number of his clients grew, Paul hired some part-timers to help out in the converted garage he used for his agency. "First an artist and layout specialist," he recalls, "and then somebody to go out and drum up new accounts."

At this point, did Paul elect to go full-time? No, he had some other cards up his sleeve. "Another of my longtime dreams was to invest in rental real estate—apartment houses, to be specific. I plunked down $1500 on a small three-family building and started devoting my free time to fixing it up. This required adding another employee to my advertising agency payroll—but I wanted to get the 'landlord' experience with an eye to bigger and better things."

Bigger and better things were not long in coming. The success of Paul's first renovation project increased the value of the building so much that he was able to buy a much larger structure from the proceeds of selling the first one.

And now Paul owns rental real estate that nets him $750 a week. What about his advertising agency? It nets nearly as much. His job? He's long since left it.

Looking back, it's obvious that Paul could have quit his job almost at the outset of either one of his money-making projects. But he didn't know it at the time, and the regular paycheck from his employer gave him the courage to carry out his dreams.

DOES IT EVER PAY TO START FULL-TIME?

That's a question I'm often asked. And, of course, the answer is yes. Many businesses have been started full-time, and a lot of them have been eminently successful. But such enterprises are beyond the scope of this book.

Some businesses that were started full-time could have been launched on a part-time basis, however. The only difference is in the level at which you start. Take mail order as an example. If you have enough money, you can rent a warehouse, stock it with products, buy full-page ads in national magazines and maybe some spots on television, and wait for the dollars to roll in.

On the other hand, you can do as I recommend in Chapter 6 and start on a limited-capital basis, building your business less rapidly but more solidly. You may eventually have a warehouse stocked with products, and you may eventually be buying full-page ads in national magazines—but only after your tried-and-proven techniques have brought you to that point. This way, the odds are much more in your favor.

THE TIME IS NOW

Another great advantage of starting on a part-time basis is that you can get started right now. Too many people with dreams of going into business for themselves put it off. They spend their lives dreaming but rarely, if ever, achieving.

There's an old proverb that states, "One of these days is none of these days." Sadly, that is the truth concerning millions of people with perfectly good business ideas who elect to procrastinate.

If you start part-time and with limited capital, you don't have to wait for "one of these days." By following my guidance you can:

- Avoid the need for a big investment.
- Hold on to your present job.
- Work the hours that are convenient for you.
- Pick a money-maker that you really enjoy.
- Grow in size as you grow in confidence.
- Overcome the inertia that's been holding you back.

Two of the items listed above deserve some special comment. Let's take a brief look at inertia and enjoyment.

DON'T LET INERTIA HOLD YOU BACK

At various points in our lives, all of us have been held back by inertia. Each of us has had what seemed like good ideas—only to procrastinate and then see someone else profit from the very same idea.

It's happened to me a number of times. I won't give details because I don't want to sound as if I'm claiming that it was really me who invented the Hula Hoop or pocket calculators or the safety pin. But several of the ideas that I kept putting off for "one of these days" were ultimately carried out by someone else.

I don't regret these instances because they taught me an important lesson. And these cases of procrastination have been offset by a number of happy successes in my life—the results of thoughtful but prompt action.

So please take this advice:

Mark the day that you began thoughtfully reading this book as the first day of your new wealth-building career—and follow up your reading with immediate action based on what you have learned.

If you do this, you will have overcome what must be the greatest obstacle to personal wealth success—inertia.

ENJOY YOUR MONEY-MAKING PROJECT

For a part-time business to be successful, it has to be fun. After all, there's no Simon Legree-type boss standing over your shoulder making sure that you get the work done on time. You are your own boss, and unless you enjoy what you're doing, you're not going to get it done on time and you're not going to do it well.

Enjoyment, then, is another of the criteria on which you should base the selection of your type of business. I pointed out earlier that many times in the course of reading this book you'll come across business plans that prompt you to exclaim, "Why, I could do that!" But that isn't enough. You should also be able to say, "Why, I'd really have fun doing that!"

As you follow the step-by-step instructions related to the particular business plan, picture yourself carrying them out. This is a time when you are allowed to daydream. Sit back in a chair and mentally put yourself into the business you are considering. Think of all the tasks involved. Think of the time they'd take. Envision the inconveniences they might sometimes cause. Think of carrying out these duties week after week. Don't think about the profits. Just think about the work.

Does the project still sound like fun? If not, continue reading until you find one that does. You have a big field to choose from.

2

Produce Profitable Products at Home

You've probably always known that it's possible to earn some money by making things at home and then selling them. What you may not have known is how much money really can be made. In fact, many people who are busily engaged in producing products at home don't realize this because they haven't yet latched on to the big profit techniques.

Fortunately, there are quite a few home-based entrepreneurs who have uncovered those techniques—and these are the people who will be showing us what to do in this chapter.

THE DEMAND FOR HOME-PRODUCED PRODUCTS

Why do consumers shell out good money for items made by individuals working at home when so many mass-produced items are already available in the marketplace, and often at lower prices?

There are a number of reasons:
- There is a huge demand for individual craftsmanship.
- Many home-made products are unusual and thus are hard to get elsewhere.
- Products produced at home can often be personalized for in-

dividual customers—something not normally possible with items coming off an assembly line.

- Quality home-made items can sometimes be cheaper because it costs big factories a lot of money to re-tool for new products.
- Since home-made items are based on the producer's own abilities and experience, superior quality is possible with no outlay for "research and development."
- Home-produced items are frequently fabricated out of natural materials that are not easily handled by automated machines.

We'll be listing a lot of profitable items that you can produce—and you'll also be keyed in on the special techniques that can convert these items into big money-makers for you. But right now, as an example of what you can do in whatever field you choose, let's look at one person's success.

HOW $1,250 LEADS TO $500,000 IN TWO YEARS

The first item on the product list later in this chapter is Assembly Kits, and that's how Ralph B. made his fortune. In his home business, Ralph really didn't manufacture anything—all he did was buy parts from various wholesalers, pack them together into a box, and include a set of instructions on how the buyer could put them together into a functioning product.

Various companies are selling assembly kits of everything from airplanes to zoom lenses, and I will let you in on a little secret. Many of the kit companies themselves don't manufacture the parts for their kits. All they do is buy parts from other companies and include an inexpensive assembly manual.

Ralph saw this as a nearly perfect way to start a home-based business, because after his product had been chosen, suppliers located, and the instruction sheets written and reproduced at a local quick print shop, very little work was left to do. All that was needed was to pack the ingredients and ship them off to waiting customers who had ordered the kits by mail.

PRODUCT SELECTION MADE EASY

Choosing a product to market in kit form was easy for Ralph, as it will be for you if you happen to choose this money-making method. He based it on his personal experience.

Ralph is an electronics hobbyist. Great strides have been made in electronics in recent years, bringing prices way down. For example, the pocket calculator that sold a few years ago for over $100 now retails for less than $10.

So, whenever new electronic gadgets hit the market, hobbyist Ralph usually had to have one. And when home computers became available at low cost, he was naturally among the first to jump on the bandwagon.

In the early years of home computers, they were sold in kit form—none were pre-assembled. After assembling the first kit he bought, Ralph realized that he could come up with something better.

"At first it was merely for my own enjoyment. Home computers are based on an inexpensive central processing unit about the size of my thumb that retails for less than $15. Although this is the 'brains' of the computer, it's what you do with the other components installed around it that determines how well your computer works."

HELP FROM BIG MANUFACTURERS

Ralph wrote to the manufacturer of the central processing unit and obtained specification sheets and design literature. Using this material as a guide, he spent a month of evenings at his home workbench and came up with a small home computer that outperformed the kit he had bought.

"Since home computing was a new hobby then, I designed it as a rather simple machine that would teach computer principles to the people who were just beginning to get interested in the hobby. It consisted of one circuit board and a power supply. The parts cost under $50. I soon realized that I could sell this same thing in kit form for about $300, and that's what I did."

Your line of kits—if that is the field you choose—may not be nearly as technical or sophisticated as Ralph's, but there's a lot to be learned from how he went about setting up his business. The business principles involved in selling sewing kits apply equally to electronic kits.

EASY BUSINESS EXPANSION

In this chapter you'll learn a number of ways to expand a home-based production business so that it brings in the big money you desire. In producing assembly kits, this is particularly easy.

Ralph explains, "Once my initial kit had been designed, the parts located, and the instructions printed, it took very little of my time to fill the orders. So adding other kits to my 'line' was a natural and almost painless thing to do. And, of course, I did it."

One by one, Ralph added the following kits:

1. Memory boards to make the computer more powerful
2. Accessories (known in the computer field as peripherals) to make the computer more useful
3. A larger and completely self-contained home computer

This is the great advantage of selling assembly kits (and, in fact, many other home-produced items): You can sell additional items to the same customers. If your products are sold mainly by mail, you have a complete record of every customer's name and address. It's easy to let your customers know of the new things you are offering.

FROM PART-TIME TO FULL-TIME

It would be a safe guess to say that Ralph was not a part-timer in the kit business for very long. In just six months, his sales and profit volume was more than he had dreamed of, and he left his job as a bank clerk to devote full-time to his business. This was at about the time that he was beginning to introduce new products.

"And not long after that," he reports, "I moved the venture out of my house to a rented warehouse located only a few miles away. I began to hire employees to help out, and as the trend switched from home computer kits to pre-assembled home computers, I was ready to make the move."

Ralph now sells one basic computer that can be bought in kit or pre-assembled form, along with a number of peripherals. Some peripherals are made in his warehouse-plant and he buys some ready-made from other manufacturers.

Ralph notes, "Once you have a sufficient number of satisfied customers you can sell them related items regardless of whether or not you make those items yourself."

Ralph recently turned down an offer from another company that wanted to buy his firm for $500,000 cash. That's quite a jump from his initial investment of $1,250.

$1,250? I can hear you asking it now: "How can a business worth $500,000 in just two years have been started with so little?"

Pay close heed to the techniques Ralph used. Some of them will be invaluable to you regardless of the type of home production venture you launch—kit or non-kit.

FROM A SHOESTRING TO A FORTUNE

In relating Ralph's experience, I've already alluded to some of the money-saving techniques he used. But let's tell the full story. Here's what he did:

1. He based his product on his own hobby interest, so no money was spent in learning the field.
2. The ingredients were inexpensive and easy to obtain.
3. He did not need to buy any major equipment in order to produce or package his product.
4. He utilized data and advice freely available from his parts suppliers.
5. He did not at first manufacture any of the parts himself.

But there's more. You may have noticed that no mention has been made so far of the cost of selling his product. If you've had any experience at all in business, you know that the sales-cost is a prime expense. In sales by direct mail, for example, advertising is almost always the Number One expense.

So how did Ralph manage that on an investment of $1,250? Let's continue our list:

6. Knowing that hobby publications are constantly writing up new products, Ralph notified each of them of his computer kit, enclosing a photograph. Several publications asked for, and received, samples to test. The products became the subject of large write-ups.
7. As for actual paid advertising, Ralph let his customers foot most of the bill. The early write-ups and his initial $300 magazine ad brought in enough money to finance a continued and expanded advertising campaign.

It is common practice when new products are developed to offer them for sale before they are actually ready to be shipped. This is particularly true in the home computer field. Many manufacturers used cash-with-orders to finance the completion of their product development.

Ralph didn't have to do this. His product was basically simple (for him), and it was ready to go immediately. Where the cash-with-orders did help him was in the advertising. It gave him the start he needed. You know the rest of the story—all $500,000 worth.

MANY FIELDS TO CHOOSE FROM

I've spent a lot of time telling you about Ralph B.'s experience for several reasons. First, many of the techniques he employed will be useful to you regardless of the home production field you choose. Second, his story illustrates how profitable such a business can become. And third, it proves an important point: In the home production field you should stick to what you already know.

In starting a production business at home, whether it features kits or souvenirs, your early goals should be:

1. To produce the best product you possibly can
2. To begin making money as soon as possible
3. To produce your items as easily as you can

By basing your product choice on a field you are already familiar with, you can accomplish these goals. There are so many fields to choose from that you should have little difficulty in finding a specialty right down your alley.

It would be impossible to list everything that can profitably be made at home. But the 50 items I have chosen to include will provide a good idea of what is selling successfully right now. Some of the listings are general and non-specific in nature. (Assembly Kits is an example. There are hundreds of types of kits you could sell.) In such cases, I've included some comments to help you decide if there's something in your particular background that makes the listing something you should seriously consider. Many of the listings are more specific and can be completely understood without any additional comment from me.

Afterwards, I'll help you decide which of the listings is best for you. Then come the step-by-step instructions on getting your home production business started and running.

50 PROFITABLE PRODUCTS

Here are 50 of the most profitable products being produced at home today. Pick one of these, follow it up with the big-profit success techniques that come later in the chapter, and you're well on your way to meeting your income goals. But don't select your specialty right away. The step-by-step instructions that come later in the chapter will provide more information to help in making your choice.

Assembly Kits: As we've already noted, there are hundreds of items to choose from. What's your hobby? See how you can adapt Ralph B.'s techniques.

Bookends: Not just any bookends, but ones that (1) are made of unusual materials, (2) depict something unusual, or (3) are souvenirs of a locale. Examples are bookends made of water-worn wood washed up on shore, or decoupaged with a colorful scene, or made of a locally available natural resource, such as Vermont's granite.

Calligraphy: Tom C. is an expert penman and he makes money producing plaques and scrolls that depict important events in his customers' lives.

Candle Specialties: Go into any hobby or craft shop and you'll get loads of ideas.

Candy Products: These are excellent mail order items because most of them don't spoil. You might also sell them to specialty stores, or as fund-raising items for non-profit organizations.

Custom Banners: Politicians, businessmen, athletic teams, special events promoters—they're all among your prospects.

Custom-Made Clothing

Decorative Gourds

Decorative Trays

Decoupage: The skill of laminating printed material to fine wood can be profitable for the person who doesn't do what most other decoupagers are doing. Pretty pictures are nice, but why not do custom work? Specialties might include diplomas, photo portraits, personal credos, business slogans, or memorable documents.

Dollhouses & Furniture

Dolls

Draperies

Dried Floral Arrangements

Exotic Foods: Make sure they're not spoilable and can be shipped easily. Also check health regulations.

Framed Posters

Fruitcakes

Glass Figurines: If your hobby is glass-blowing and you're good at it, you can sell to gift shops. Then enlist other hobbyists to expand your production.

Handbags: Make them of vinyl or leather—but make them unusual so that you can compete with the mass-produced stuff. Made-to-order work does exceptionally well.

Handcrafted Jewelry

Handpainted Dishes

Home Baking: This doesn't mean selling pies and cakes to the neighbors. It does mean making a production center out of your kitchen, selling items of home-baked quality to stores and restaurants. That's the way Margaret Rudkin started Pepperidge Farm. A number of others have achieved outstanding success in a similar manner.

Hooked Rugs

House Signs: In this age when everyone is known by his or her Social Security, charge card, telephone, or street number, people crave unique means of personal identification. Hence the demand for attractive name signs that can be attached to homes or spiked into front lawns.

Imitation Flower Arrangements

Lawn Decorations: These also appeal to people who seek to assert their individualism. When 30 homes in a development all look alike, it's the landscaping and lawn decor that set one home apart from another.

Leather Goods

Macramé

Mass-Produced Art: If you like business as much as art—and you're good at both—this could be the plan for you. The market for real paintings (not reproductions) to hang in homes and offices has never been greater. Many artists have developed techniques for turning out attractive pictures at a rapid clip, thus making them affordable to the masses. As you grow, assign more of the work to other artists. Chapter 10 has a lot of ideas on making money in art.

Metalworking

Mosaics

Nameplates for Boats: People who have spent thousands of dollars for their pleasure boats are justifiably proud of these possessions. That's why they often shell out quite a lot of money for distinctive nameplates to attach to the sterns.

Natural Food Products: You can buy them wholesale and sell them retail. It's a giant of an industry, and a field in which you can start on a mail order basis working out of your home. With all the additives in junk supermarket foods these days, there's a tremendous market for natural foods.

Novelty Items: You've been making little doodads for the children or grandchildren. And neighbors have been clamoring for these items for their children. If this sounds familiar, then you may have the start of a real money-making home production project.

Personalized Welcome Mats

Pet Breeding: To some people, a "pet factory" has evil connotations—but do it right, aiming for quality, and you can win a good business reputation as well as a big income. Since animals are self-reproducing, you can start with a minimal investment and grow naturally. And you need not be limited to dogs and cats. Billy R. sells everything from fish to snakes, airmailing them all over the country from his New Jersey outlet.

Planters

Pottery

Regional Foods: Sell them to tourists, through local stores, through the mail direct to the consumer, or through other mail order companies.

Restored Antiques: Some people want to buy antiques and restore them themselves, while others want them in tiptop shape to begin with. There's a big market serving the second category of antique-lovers.

Rough-Hewn Walking Sticks: The raw material—small tree limbs—is available almost everywhere. The finished, polished product is easy to produce and is a good seller in gift shops.

Silverwork

Souvenirs for Tourists

Specialty Lamps: Almost anything can be made into lampbases. Jan M. runs a lamp shop in a resort area and also ships her unusual merchandise all across the country.

Stoneware Kitchen Items

Stuffed Animals

Wall Mottoes

Weathervanes

Wicker Baskets

Wooden Furniture

HOW TO PICK YOUR PRODUCT

You shouldn't pick your product right now. Even if you've spotted something in the list that really appeals to you, keep an open mind until you've read the step-by-step instructions on starting a home production center.

And even if you haven't come across something in the list that seems feasible as a money-making project at first glance, you should still finish reading the chapter. There are two reasons:

1. You may discover while reading the instructions that conducting one of the businesses can be a lot easier than you expected; the unusual profit methods and profit potential may spark renewed interest.

2. Even if you have no interest in starting and running a home production center, many of the business and promotional methods can be applied to the type of business you eventually do decide upon.

What happens after you have read the instructions and have decided that producing products at home is for you? Which product line should you pick? I've already given you a few tips on this, but right now I'll include them in a list of factors you should consider.

- Choose a field you already know. This way you can get your production started almost instantly. You'll also be familiar with the appeal of, and demand for, the product. This is not to imply that you can't pick an item that is a variation of something you already know. Take rough-hewn walking sticks as an example. You may never have made one in your life, but you may have worked with rough wood. That's sufficient. A number of the items are easy to learn about provided you have a general knowledge of the type of work involved.

- Select an item you know will sell. How do you determine this? By sending away for and examining catalogs, visiting gift shops, and studying the magazine ads. When you see a particular type of item over and over again, you know people are already making good money at it, and there's probably room for your product in the marketplace.

- Make sure that the raw materials are readily available. Without them, you can't do much production or make much money.

- Determine how much time it will take to make the product,

using efficient one-person production-line methods (as explained in the forthcoming instructions). Make sure you can charge enough to be adequately paid for your time and receive a generous profit. Merely being paid for your time is not good enough: if that's all you want, get a part-time job. It's the profit that counts.

• Don't overlook the enjoyment factor. As you start in business, you'll be doing most if not all of the work yourself. To do it well you must like doing it. Later, others will probably be doing most of the work for you, but it doesn't make sense to start out in a business you don't enjoy.

Bear in mind that the 50 items in our listing are merely guidelines. Reading through the list several times and on several different occasions may lead you to think of other product items that match your ability and experience even more closely.

A STEP-BY-STEP GUIDE TO STARTING AND RUNNING YOUR PRODUCTION BUSINESS

There are six key steps involved in starting and running your own home production business. I'll list them first and then we'll discuss each step individually. Here are the steps:

1. Build and test your product
2. Develop efficient production-line techniques
3. Choose a sales method and test it
4. Put your product on the market
5. Have others take over the work
6. Consider going full-time

Now let's see how you can carry out each of these steps and build a home-based money-making venture from scratch.

STEP ONE:
Build and Test Your Product

Every manufacturing company, large or small, begins with what is called a prototype. Building one, or a few, of the items you plan to sell tells you right off whether the end-product is as good as you had pictured it. If not, you have the opportunity to refine and improve it.

Here are some examples from my files:

- When Peggy L. decided to go into the home bakeshop business, her plan was to sell cakes and pies to restaurants so that they could offer their patrons "home-made" desserts. Peggy had made cakes and pies all her life, but until now she hadn't worried about the cost of ingredients. By experimenting in her kitchen, she was able to substitute certain less expensive ingredients that did not affect the flavor or freshness. She went through a half dozen prototypes before settling on her final products.

- Before amateur dog-breeders Stan and Dot N. decided to "go public" with their German Shepherds, they bred several of their females with a number of stud dogs until they arrived at the breed line they sought. "We wanted to sell dogs bred for looks and temperament, and we achieved our goal," this couple reports. Their puppies sell for a minimum of $400 each, and the business has become a real profit-maker.

- Boating enthusiast Andy F. had an idea for unusual nameplates that other boatmen could install on the sterns of their craft. The names would be burnished in wood to give a rustic effect. "Luckily I didn't go full speed ahead with my plan," Andy notes. "First I made a prototype for my own boat. Before the season was over I discovered that the type of wood I had chosen was not standing up well under the rigors of the marine atmosphere." Having learned an important lesson from his prototype, Andy switched to redwood, a much more stable product. He's built a sizable business selling the nameplates at boat shows and through the mail.

You can see from these examples that there are three chief reasons for building and testing a prototype product:

1. You want to be certain that a good product can be produced inexpensively enough to return a profit.
2. You want the product to be of true value to the purchaser.
3. You want to be sure that the product will continue to be of value to the consumer long after it has been purchased.

It may take two, three, or even more prototypes until you have arrived at your ultimate model. You'll find the effort has been well worthwhile.

STEP TWO:
Develop Efficient Production-Line Techniques

Producing one or two prototypes and producing hundreds or even thousands of duplicate items are two entirely separate processes. Once your prototype has been developed to your complete satisfaction, you should strive to develop methods that will allow you to produce the item with as much efficiency as possible.

This means using production-line techniques even while you remain a one-person shop. The techniques that save a lot of time and trouble for you now will be even more valuable later when you may add workers to your operation.

"But I thought people were attracted to individually-produced items because of their craftsmanship," a budding businesswoman remarked to me recently. "If I start using those production-line techniques you speak about, won't that appeal be lost?"

Not at all. The only thing such methods do is improve your efficiency. They should have no effect on the quality of the product. An illustration of this is provided by the experience of Bob W., who makes wooden lawn furniture.

"I never make a piece of furniture from beginning to end, in that order," Bob explains. "Instead, I may spend one evening cutting out pieces, the next evening putting them together, and the third and fourth applying the finish. I've found that this allows me to produce the items far more rapidly than if I were to go from one task to another and back again."

Such production-line techniques can be used in almost any type of product you might choose. These are some other examples from my files:

- A leather goods producer in the West cuts his pieces during one work period, spends the next period sewing, and devotes the third to applying whatever stains or decorative materials are called for.
- A producer of stuffed animals in New England follows the same process—except that her business has now grown to the point where she is "farming out" much of the work. Several women in the community cut cloth for her in their own homes, while other ladies are involved in sewing. "This way I can devote most of my

efforts to selling the items through the mail and to gift and novelty shops," she reports.

- In a New Jersey seashore community, a man who makes souvenirs for tourists has a product line that includes several different items. He uses production-line techniques for each. And as he developed these techniques, he "timed out" each process. This means that he kept a record of how much work was accomplished during each work period, and of how many products the work resulted in. Dividing the number of products by the number of hours, he arrived at a figure showing him how long it took to produce each item.

It's important to do as the New Jersey man did and determine how much time it takes to produce your products. This will be a factor in setting your prices. Basically, your prices will be determined by four factors:

1. Cost of materials
2. Your time
3. Overhead
4. Your profit

An explanation of two of the items is in order. The overhead includes not only such things as electricity and incidental supplies, but also selling costs. Depending on the nature of the product, this can be the largest single expense. If you sell through the mail, for example, selling cost can account for as much as half the retail price of the product.

Let me stress again that when it comes to profit, don't think for a moment that merely paying yourself for the hours you put in is enough. If all you're going to do is get paid for your time, then you might as well go to work for somebody else and let that person assume the problems and risks of running a business. The reason anybody goes into business is to earn a *profit*—and that should be over and above the generous hourly rate you pay yourself.

STEP THREE:
Choose a Sales Method and Test It

Home-produced items are sold in many different ways:
- Through gift shops
- In home shops
- To department stores

- At flea markets
- To restaurants
- Through the mail
- At tourist stands
- At crafts shows
- To mail order houses
- On consignment to dealers

Chapter 6 of this book deals with mail order and will provide you with insight on how to sell your products that way. Much can also be learned by a thorough reading of Chapter 8, which deals with high-profit sales techniques.

Regardless of which method you choose, it should be tested before you put your plan into full swing. To illustrate why, we again go to my files:

- Pete K., who spent many weekends and most vacations in a rural farm area, noticed while attending farm auctions that many old wagon wheels could be purchased inexpensively. Realizing that back home in his suburban community people were using wagon wheels for decorative purposes, he began buying up a supply. Then, at home, he painted them in appealing colors. Appealing to him, that is, but apparently not to potential customers. "I found that buyers wanted them in their original unpainted form," he reports. Happily, he had not painted up very many of his "prototypes" before making this discovery. Now he sells the wheels "as is" and makes excellent money for a minimum amount of work.

- Joan T. fashions walking sticks out of rough-hewn wood. Her initial idea was to sell the sticks to mail order houses, but although a few companies ordered test lots, the walking sticks did not sell satisfactorily. "That's apparently because people have to see them and handle them to appreciate them," Joan reasons. Now they are sold through gift shops, which sell all that Joan and her helpers can produce.

The moral of these and other experiences I could cite is that you should devote as much effort to testing sales methods as you have devoted to developing and testing your product. Don't lose sight of the fact that any desirable product can be sold provided you use the right method.

"Fine," you say, "I'll test my sales method when I choose it. But how do I go about choosing it in the first place?"

There's a simple rule that answers this question. It is so simple that some people might be fooled into thinking that it's not effective. But it works, and you'll see why. Here's the rule:

> *The first method you should test for selling your product is the same method used by the majority of those who already sell similar products.*

The reason for this is just as simple as the method itself. If a number of other companies use the same method, it is proven effective! Think about it for a moment. If you see items similar to yours in gift shop after gift shop, then you know they must be selling there. If you consistently see them advertised for sale through the mail, then you know that direct mail is a proven sales method for that particular product.

"But what," you ask, "if my product is highly unusual? What if nothing exactly like it is sold anywhere else?"

Your action in that case is to determine how items of similar appeal, if not precisely the same in style or content, are most frequently sold. Thus, if you are producing rough-hewn walking sticks and you've never spotted another one for sale anywhere, then look for the closest thing you can find. Had Joan T., in the example given above, followed this rule, she probably would never have attempted to sell her walking sticks through mail order houses. She would have noticed that ornamental canes (the closest thing to rough-hewn walking sticks commonly available) are often found in gift shops but less frequently in mail order catalogs.

STEP FOUR:
Put Your Product on the Market

The questions I'm most frequently asked by people who are interested in selling products that they produce at home are these:

"I know how I want to sell the product, but I don't know whom to contact. How can I get in touch with dealers and stores and mail order houses across the country? How do I know when crafts-oriented shows and flea markets are scheduled? How can I learn about trade shows worth attending?"

The answer to all these questions is that you should subscribe to and regularly read the trade magazines. In fact, this is something you should do no matter what business you enter. The only way to keep current on markets and trends is to learn what others in various parts of the country are doing. And in the crafts field, there are a number of publications and directories to help you.

The following magazines may be available at your local library, or can be subscribed to by writing to these addresses:

> *Craft, Model and Hobby Industry*
> Hobby Publishing Inc.
> 225 W. 34th St.
> New York, NY 10001

> *The Crafts Report*
> 700 Orange St.
> Wilmington, DE 19801

> *Creative Crafts*
> PO Box 700
> Newton, NJ 07860

Directories that can be helpful to you in locating and choosing your markets include these:

> *Annual Craft, Model & Hobby Industry Directory*
> Hobby Publishing Inc.
> 225 W. 34th St.
> New York, NY 10001

> *Contemporary Crafts Marketplace*
> R.R. Bowker
> Ann Arbor, MI 48106

And finally, you may want to consider joining a professional organization or two, such as:

> *Hobby Industry Association of America*
> 200 Fifth Ave.
> New York, NY 10010

> *National Crafts Association*
> 6116 N. Central Expressway
> Dallas, TX 75206

STEP FIVE:
Have Others Take Over the Work

The time will come when you will be selling all you can produce and will have to turn down additional orders. This is when you should consider turning at least part of the workload over to others. It's a step many people hesitate to take because they fear being saddled with a regular payroll to meet. But it can be a painless process if you go at it the right way.

Most or even all of what you are doing can be farmed out to others on a piecework basis. You can skip the bother of making payroll deductions, etc. All you do—at least initially—is pay other people to perform the work in their own homes. They are considered contractors; they are not your employees.

Felix Q.'s business is making and selling wall mottoes. Although he still does the actual engraving himself, he has a number of woodworkers in his community cut out the plaques for him from wood that he supplies, and a neighbor does the finishing.

"This way I do only the work that requires my special attention," Felix comments. "I do the unusual engraving that has made my mottoes best-sellers in a number of gift catalogs and gift departments of department stores." And, of course, being freed of the routine chores, Felix can devote more of his time to administrative and sales duties.

Depending on the nature of your product, when the time comes to farm out some of the work, it might be more practical to send it to commercial firms that are in business for that purpose. Vincent B. developed a thriving enterprise making custom banners for political parties, caterers, businessmen, and convention sponsors. The business thrived so well, in fact, that the orders soon far surpassed his ability to produce. Now he actually farms out the entire banner-production process to commercial firms.

"I continue to design the banners," Vincent reports, "and because of my knowledge of where I can get special types of work done—and done on schedule—I continue to be inundated with orders."

STEP SIX:
Consider Going Full-Time

Another question I'm frequently asked deals with the point at which a person should consider giving up a regular job to devote full-time to the production and sale of his or her product. Generally, I've found that if you have to ask the question, then you're probably not yet ready. Here are some of the signs that will let you know you're ready:

1. You probably will have set up a production facility outside your home; or most of the production work is being handled by outsiders.

2. Your net profit will be at least equal to what you earn from your regular job.

3. You are fully confident that devoting full-time to the project will increase sales and profits significantly.

I've also found that most people who are ready to go full-time have become restless in their regular jobs. They can't wait to go home at the end of the regular workday and get started on their second income project. They find the challenges and the rewards of the spare-time business a lot more satisfying.

These are the people who are ready to make the big switch. You'll know it when the time comes.

But there's another thing you should know—and this is a wonderful aspect of starting and running a spare-time business. You don't ever have to go full-time if you don't want to. It's entirely up to you. You're the boss. You can hold the business down to a size that fits comfortably into your available spare-time hours or you can allow it to grow to its full potential, and perhaps become rich doing so.

3

Earn Top Dollar with Repairs and Maintenance

America's fastest-growing industry is the service industry, and one of the largest segments of that industry is repairs and maintenance. In fact, the U.S. Commerce Department reports that in the coming decade, services will provide the country's largest area of economic growth.

So if you want to get in on a boom-times industry and draw the big money that comes when demand far outstrips the supply, look into repairs and maintenance.

HOW $700 BRINGS A $750 WEEKLY INCOME

An example of the type of low-investment business that can be developed is the one started by Kevin C., who chose R&M (repairs and maintenance) because he couldn't afford to do much else. As it turned out, he couldn't have done much better.

"Frankly," Kevin says, "I was deeply in debt. We had bought a new home and found, after my wife had to leave work to have our first child, that it was getting almost impossible to meet the mortgage payments. I looked around for a way to make some extra money and then I spotted an ad for a second-hand floor polisher in the newspaper's classified section."

The polishing machine was available for $300, and when he went to look at it he found that the seller actually had two available.

"I was able to borrow the $600 from my father-in-law, and I bought both machines," he recalls. "I wanted two so that I'd always have one available if the other broke down. Also, my father-in-law was willing to help out if I got more work than I could handle."

Kevin went to a quick print shop and had some circulars printed. He mailed them to businesses in and around his home town, and he also ordered a regular ad in the "Services" column of his newspaper. The advertising cost came to $60. That, along with $40 for incidental supplies, brought the investment to $700.

SERVICE DOLLARS ROLL IN

"It's a good thing I bought the two machines," Kevin reports. "I quickly found that there was more business than I could possibly handle alone in my spare time. My father-in-law was a big help, but it soon became evident that it was more than even the two of us could handle."

What did Kevin do? With the profits that had begun to roll in, he bought some more machines (new this time) and inserted some more ads in the newspaper.

"More ads?" you inquire. No, not ads for more business—ads for part-timers to run the machines.

"It was easy to get people to work for me," Kevin reports. "Most floor maintenance work is done on nights and weekends when offices and factories are closed, and this is precisely when a lot of people are available to work."

With a dozen people now on call when he needs them, Kevin is running a business that nets him $750 a week.

"And a great thing about it," he notes, "is that I rarely, if ever, go out on the job myself anymore. My wife takes the business calls during the day while I'm at my regular job, and I work an hour or two each evening at my desk and on the phone handling the administrative details."

His mortgage? "That problem was quickly resolved. In fact, I now have a bigger mortgage. The success of my business has allowed us to move into a larger home in a better part of town."

THE WORLD IS CRYING OUT FOR QUALITY SERVICE

When you decide to start a spare-time repair and maintenance business, you have a lot going for you:

- It's one of the easiest fields to enter.
- The demand for R&M services is constantly growing.

• The profit margin is unusually high.

Let's take a look at each of these three factors and see how you can benefit by choosing an R&M specialty that matches your background and experience.

AN EASY FIELD TO ENTER

Often, all it takes to set yourself up in a lucrative R&M business are a few simple hand tools. Or, as in the case of Kevin C., a specialized piece of equipment might be required—but any of the 50 badly-needed R&M businesses featured in this chapter can be launched with a total investment of less than $1,500.

Knowledge and training? Many fields require no specialized training at all, just a few hours of "hands-on" experience. Kevin had never operated a buffing machine before, but his lack of experience certainly did not hold him back.

There are, of course, a number of fields where specialized knowledge is required. Perhaps you'll pick a field that is in line with work you've done in your regular job. Or, if you spot a special need in your community for a service that doesn't match your present abilities, it might pay to take a course or two to learn the rudiments. More on this later.

You don't have to rent a store or shop to impress customers. It's your service they're after—not your surroundings. The work you perform will be done at either of two locations:

1. In your own home, in the work area you have set aside.
2. "On location" at the customer's home or place of business.

You probably will need a car, van, or pickup truck. But many R&M business operators, as they start out in business, use their personal vehicles. Later, as the amount of business and profit warrants, they sometimes require a business vehicle.

CONSTANTLY GROWING DEMAND

The demand never seems to stop growing for most types of repair and maintenance services. This is partly because we live in an era of mechanization. Businesses and individuals depend increasingly on tools and appliances to handle a great part of their workloads. All of these tools and appliances require repair and maintenance.

Finding someone to do the R&M work that you need when you

need it is getting to be quite a problem today. You've probably experienced this yourself, the last time the hi-fi broke down or the caned seat broke in an antique chair. Chances are that the companies you contacted were willing to accept you as customers, provided you didn't mind being put on a waiting list. Or perhaps you were lucky enough to find someone who was able to do the job immediately, provided you took the item to his shop located some 50 miles away.

Pick one of the "growth" service fields listed in this chapter (basing your choice on the criteria also listed in this chapter) and you can cash in on the ever increasing need for R&M services.

ENJOY UNUSUALLY HIGH PROFITS

There are two important reasons why your profit margin in an R&M business can be substantially higher than in many other fields:

1. People don't usually "bargain-hunt" when it comes to services. They need the service and they need it now, so they're willing to pay any reasonable charge without quibbling.
2. Often there is a double-barreled profit. You charge not only for your time and expertise, but also for any replacement parts you may install. And you get the full list price for those parts.

Irv J. has profited handsomely because of these two factors. His spare-time business, launched several years ago, is involved in repairing intercom and paging systems that are used in offices and factories.

"Businesses don't want to give up such equipment for the length of time it takes to send it back to the factory for service there," Irv explains, "so I found loads of customers when I first announced my service."

Irv keeps the average piece of equipment for only a day or two (if, indeed, he has to remove it from the premises at all) and customers happily pay the $17.50 per hour labor charge he imposes. As for parts (transistors, integrated circuits, speakers, and the like), they pay the full list price.

"In most cases, my customers would be able to buy the same parts at a substantial discount at a local electronics store, but then they would have to install them. Most business people don't know how and don't want to be bothered if they do know how. They call me, and all of us benefit."

Even though his repair service is still a part-time affair as far as Irv is concerned, it has become a full-time business. That's because he manages it in his spare time while holding down a regular job—but he also has a full-time technician working for him now. His business netted him $22,000 last year.

50 BADLY NEEDED REPAIR AND MAINTENANCE SPECIALTIES

What kind of repair and maintenance business can you start and run with less than $1,500? As you'll see, the list is quite comprehensive. And each of the businesses on the list is there because it is a "today" service—one that meets a growing demand in today's society.

You may or may not see a business on the list for which you are instantly qualified. Remember, many of the fields are easily learned; and where special training is required, the profit potential in your community may make such training more than worthwhile. We'll be discussing this aspect later. But for now, let's look at some of today's hottest opportunities in the service field.

Air Conditioner Repairs and Installation: People tinker with their own cars and TV sets but they almost never tackle an air conditioner. They send out for help, and you can be the help they send for if you have either the experience or the training.

Antennas: Climbing roofs to install TV or communications antennas is something most people don't want to be bothered with. That's why companies specializing in this kind of work do so well.

Antiques Restoration: Furniture refinishing in itself can be a profitable field; refinishing and restoring antiques can be even more profitable because the items you work on are more valuable to begin with and people are willing to spend more to get them back in shape.

Appliances

Art Restoration: Many people have treasured paintings that either are faded or have tears. If you have, or can develop, a knack for correcting such problems, you have a ready-made business.

Auto Painting: The out-of-this-world prices of new cars are causing a lot of people to hold on to their present models longer, and this often makes a new paint job desirable. There are many abandoned service stations available for rent inexpensively, and any of these can be converted into a paint shop.

Auto Radios

Auto Tune-Ups, On Location: The convenience factor of not

having to take their cars to a garage for a tune-up or oil change has caused many people to use the services of so-called "driveway tune-up" companies. Armed with a panel truck containing the necessary tools, you can go to the customer's location and do the work on the spot.

Basement Waterproofing

Bicycles

Boats: Boat engines are very similar to car engines. If you've had experience working on car engines, then you can work with the marine variety. There is one difference: you charge more. Or, you can specialize in hull repairs. Since there are not many hull repairmen around, the money is even better.

Burglar Alarm Systems

Cameras: It usually doesn't pay to open up a camera repair shop to which customers bring their broken cameras. Instead, you can handle the repair work that is dropped off at regular camera stores. One New Yorker has a dozen camera stores on his list and has developed a thriving repair business. He started the business after taking a home study camera repair course he saw advertised in a photography magazine.

Carpet and Rug Cleaning

CB Radios

Chair Caning

Concrete: A repairman specializing in concrete? Why not? If you've ever noticed all the business and home sidewalks that need patching or even more substantial repair, you already know the need for a service business specializing in this. One entrepreneur I know of is also a bicycle enthusiast. He rides his bike through the area making note of sidewalks that need work. Later, he contacts the owners and offers his services. His business is doing quite well.

Diesel Engines: More and more vehicles, boats, and industrial machines are diesel-powered these days, and the need for specialists able to tend these fussy power sources is increasing. Many owners of diesel engines start out by having manufacturer's technicians work on their equipment; when they discover the rates that these companies charge they quickly move to a local, non-affiliated service. You can undercharge the big company competition and still profit handsomely.

Do-It-Yourself Shop: A lot of people like to work on their own cars, develop their own pictures, get involved in ceramics, etc., but don't have the facilities required. So they go to a do-it-yourself shop and rent the facilities and equipment by the hour. Set up such a shop in your own field of expertise and you can make excellent money. Virtually all do-it-yourself shops have experienced personnel standing by to provide advice for hobbyists who need it. That, and collecting the money, is your role.

Driveway Sealing

Electric Motors

Electronic Organs

Exterminating and Fumigating

Fire Alarm Systems

Fleet Vehicle Cleaning: Rig yourself a truck or van with high-pressure pumping equipment, tap in to the customer's water line, and you're in business washing fleets of trucks or cars on location.

Floor Polishing

Floor Refinishing

Formica Installation: Homeowners who don't know how to do this find it a messy and usually unsatisfactory task. Service businesses that install formica find a big demand for their work.

Furniture Cleaning

Furniture Refinishing

Garment Repairs & Alterations: You don't have to open up a tailor shop. All you need to do is arrange with a number of dry cleaning stores to handle their repairs for them. All dry cleaning shops get inquiries about repairs and alterations, but most can't afford to keep a tailor on the payroll. You can develop a route of several shops, handling all such work for them.

Heating Systems

Hi-Fi Systems

Home Cleaning: Housewives in the know don't hire "cleaning women" these days; they retain the services of home-cleaning agencies. You can set up such an agency, hiring other people to do the work for you on a part- or full-time basis. See Chapter 5 for details on how you can profit from the work of others.

House Painting

Interior Painting

Landscaping

Lawn Care

> *Locksmith*
> *Masonry*
> *Office Cleaning*
> *Office Equipment*
> *Paging and Intercom Systems*
> *Piano Tuning and Repair*
> *Power Mower, Snowblower, Garden Tractor Maintenance*
> *Saw and Blade Sharpening*
> *Small Engines*
> *Tree Service*

TV Sets: One way to make extra money doing this is to offer night and weekend service. Most TV repairmen won't go out after hours. The person who does can charge premium rates.

Window Washing: This is a job anybody can do but which most property owners don't want to do for themselves. Hire students or other part-timers to handle the task for you and you can administer a much-needed and profitable business.

HOW TO CHOOSE YOUR R&M SPECIALTY

There are two basic considerations in choosing your repair and maintenance specialty:

1. The need for the particular service in the territory you plan to cover.
2. Your ability to provide the needed service.

The importance of these two factors is in the order listed. Need is more important than ability. Why? The need either exists or it doesn't exist; you can't build it out of nothing. But ability can be acquired, and it is worthwhile to do so provided the need exists.

However, the two factors do relate to each other, as you'll see when we examine each of them.

FIND A NEED YOU CAN FILL

While you check and re-check the list of 50 badly-needed repair and maintenance specialties, you should naturally look first for types of work you know you can do with little boning up. In fact, I suggest that you take a piece of paper and jot down each of the items that you feel you could handle almost immediately. Make note of each such item even if it doesn't particularly appeal to you at the moment.

Chances are you'll have written down at least five and perhaps even ten or more R&M specialties that you could tackle with little difficulty. The next thing to do is to determine which of these services is most needed in your area.

One way to do this is to conduct what I call a Community Survey. Despite the title I've given it, it does not require going out and asking people what services they want or need. All it requires is looking through a phone book and noting which businesses are located in which communities.

Let's say that one business you're considering is electronic organ repairs. You're an electronics hobbyist and you know that fixing organs is no more difficult than fixing TV sets once you become familiar with the unique circuits used in organs.

What you do to conduct a Community Survey is check the Yellow Pages for organ repair services. Determine how many are located in each town in your area. Then find out the population of each town. Perhaps your home town has no organ repair service and has a population of 30,000. A neighboring community has two such services and a population of 35,000. And a third town, with a 20,000 population, has one organ service. It's clear that your home town is "under-serviced" when it comes to organ repairs. Other towns have one organ repair service for each 15-20,000 residents. Your town has none at all.

SURVEY THE BUSINESS NEEDS

"Yes," you say, "but how can a Community Survey tell me anything significant if what I am considering is a business service? The number of residents would have little bearing there."

That's true, and so you compare the number of potential business customers instead of community populations.

Again, let's take a hypothetical example. We'll say that you are thinking of starting an office-cleaning service. Certainly, the population of the area has little bearing on the need for this kind of business. What counts is the number of offices—and the number of competing cleaning firms.

The Community Survey in this case is conducted by going through the Yellow Pages and counting the number of firms that are likely to have sizable offices. Do this for each community in your area. Then count the number of office-cleaning firms active in each community.

When you come across a community that has a considerably higher proportion of offices compared to cleaning firms, you have found a need that probably should be filled.

Here's what your Community Survey might look like:

Community	No. of Offices	No. of Cleaning Firms
Hometown	23	1
Nextown	47	1
Newtown	25	1
Oldtown	50	2

You can see from the chart that most towns have one cleaning firm for about each 25 offices. But one community, Nextown, has far more offices per cleaning firm. Its ratio is 47 to 1. It seems to be a ripe prospect for another office-cleaning service.

It's true that business services and even home services usually pay little attention to community boundaries. In the above example, a firm headquartered in Oldtown might well be cleaning a number of offices in Nextown. That might account for the high office-to-cleaning firm ratio there. But it also indicates that there's room for somebody else to move in. The company in Oldtown probably got the customers by default; there simply was little competition.

Sometimes, of course, a Community Survey is not needed if you know from experience in the field that a service you are considering could do well. My friend, Harry A., is a case in point. He worked as a diesel mechanic in a truck shop on Long Island. The area was dotted with marinas and yacht clubs. While there was a diesel repair service in the area, he knew that many boat owners were not satisfied with its service. Also, the mechanics were not available to go out on weekends except for premium rates.

Since weekends were precisely when Harry was available, he knew that he could get loads of business from boat owners who want to be present when their engines are serviced. He was right, and he is now earning as much on weekends as he does in his regular job. He's thinking of going full-time, servicing boats in-the-water during the summer and overhauling engines in his own shop during the winter.

DO WHAT YOU KNOW OR CAN LEARN

Obviously, profits will come quicker if you can start right out in a field in which you've already had practical experience. In the example given above, Harry was already a qualified mechanic. The boat engine service was a natural for him. If you find such a "natural" service opportunity in your own line of work, that is the field you should consider.

But suppose you spot a need in your area and you don't have experience qualifying you to handle it? Give serious thought to learning the field. There are a number of ways you can do this:

1. Take special study courses.
2. Train yourself through reading and practice.
3. Take on-the-job training.

The third method may require a bit of explanation. What I mean by on-the-job training is to take a part-time job in the field. What better way to learn the ins and outs of a particular service line?

When Ed L. noticed that a carpet and rug cleaning service was needed in his area, he decided to get his training in just this way. He watched the "Help Wanted" ads in the paper until he found a firm in a nearby community that was looking for a part-timer. He went to work for that firm on his days off.

"I learned a lot more than I ever could have in a formal training school," Ed recalls. "Not only did I learn the rug cleaning methods—I also became familiar with the suppliers of cleaning products serving our area. I got to know pricing policies inside out, and I learned firsthand a number of the pitfalls to avoid."

The on-the-job training was extremely valuable to Ed. After about eight months in the part-time job, he left to form his own company. It, too, was part-time—at first. Now, some two years later, it's full-time, and earning him $35,000 a year.

A STEP-BY-STEP GUIDE TO STARTING YOUR R&M BUSINESS

As I've already noted, starting a repair and maintenance business can be one of the easiest things in the world to do. That's because:

1. If you've chosen your specialty well, the demand for your service is considerably greater than the "supply."
2. The only required investment should be for whatever tools and equipment you need, a few incidental supplies, and perhaps a bit of inexpensive advertising.
3. In most R&M specialties, the actual work can be pieced in around your full-time job and other obligations. It isn't as if you were running a retail business and had to maintain regular store hours.

This was proven by Sam K., who spotted an opportunity in his Midwestern town when an elderly piano tuner died. His death meant that the closest piano tuning service was located some 60 miles away.

"It was an opportunity with a capital 'O' even if I didn't know the first thing about pianos," Sam comments. "I recalled having seen an ad for a home study piano tuning and repair course in one of the mechanics magazines and I immediately sent away for details. The material I received indicated that the training was rather thorough and would provide me with enough practical experience to go into business for myself."

So Sam ordered the course and spent the next several months proceeding through the lessons, using the tools that were supplied with the study material. He bought several old and beat-up pianos to practice on and became quite adept at getting them in tune and in shape.

"I even made money during the training period by selling those restored pianos at a profit," he remembers.

Several months later, Sam hung out his shingle. That, a small classified ad in the newspaper, and a listing in the Yellow Pages, comprised his main advertising. "I put in a telephone answering device to take calls during the day when I was at the factory where I am employed," Sam reports. "Folks didn't seem to mind that I was only available to go to their homes on nights and weekends."

Occasionally, Sam would get two kinds of calls that were not related to actual tuning or repairs: people would inquire as to whether he had a used piano for sale, and other people would ask if he would do them the "favor" of removing an unwanted old piano.

"Usually, the pianos I was offered were in pretty poor shape, but thanks to my training and the experience I was gaining, I was able to put them back into condition so that I could sell them readily to people in search of an instrument on which their children could practice their lessons."

Thus, Sam found that dealing in used pianos became an important part of his business. It also gave him an enjoyable activity at home to keep him profitably occupied during the occasional periods when he was not needed elsewhere to do tuning.

To build up his business even further, Sam had some cards printed and he distributed them to likely "repeat" prospects—potential customers who, if satisfied, would be needing him rather often. The cards went to schools, churches, clubs and organizations that maintained recreational halls, music teachers, and nightclubs that featured regular entertainment.

The upshot is that he is now earning better than $350 a week in his business. "I'd quit my regular job right now if it weren't for the fact that I'll be eligible for early retirement in a couple of years. I'll wait until then. And after retirement, I'll expand the piano business—with a good pension to supplement my business income."

Note the switch. Many retirees seek small businesses to supplement their pensions. Sam is so successful that the business income should far surpass his pension, and thus it is the pension that will be supplemented.

HOW YOU CAN DO IT

Let's presume that you are in Sam's position and have spotted a need in your community for an R&M service. Following in his footsteps, here are the steps you should take:

1. If you lack the required training, sign up for a course, or perhaps get your training by going to work part-time for a firm that is already active in the field. Don't be concerned if the company you choose as a trainer is not located nearby. You're not going to make a career out of it; all you want is some practical experience.

2. When you're ready, take out a minimal amount of advertising—just enough to let likely prospects know you're in business and ready to serve them.

3. Also contact some likely "repeat" prospects directly. Repeat business from satisfied customers is one of the mainstays of the R&M field.

4. Look for ways to augment your R&M income. Many service specialists become dealers in the type of product they repair. Their constant contact with people who use the product (1) gives them leads on where used items can be bought cheaply, and (2) makes them the natural party for prospective purchasers to call when seeking such a product.

MONEY-MAKING TIPS FOR ANY R&M BUSINESS

When I contacted Sam recently to get the details of his success story for this book, he emphasized some of the "little extras" that have made his business consistently successful. Because these are techniques that will work in any R&M enterprise, I'll pass them on to you now:

- Because repeat business—winning the same customers over and over again—is especially important, Sam installs a sticker on each piano with his name and phone number printed on it. He also sends "reminder" cards just like dentists do when you are ready for another checkup.

- Develop a "bedside manner." Just as patients prefer friendly doctors, people hiring a serviceman want one who will talk over the problem with them in a friendly way. The person who goes right to his task without a comment may be fully proficient—but everything else being equal, his competitor is likely to get called the next time.

- Look for various ways to augment your income, not only dealing in the type of product you service, but also selling related items. Whenever Sam notices that a piano he's working on lacks a bench, he informs the customer that he has "just the right bench to go with your piano." He also sells clip-on lights that help pianists see the sheet music better.

- Guarantee your work. Offer to correct it free of charge should anything go wrong within a reasonable period of time. "People get a warm feeling of reassurance from this," Sam reports, "and you would be surprised at how rarely they take you up on it. But even when they do, that merely serves to establish you in their minds as a trustworthy businessman to be retained the next time—and one to recommend to their friends."

- Subscribe to trade publications. That's one of the best ways to keep up on what's new in your field and to learn what others in the field are doing to increase profits. Go to your public library and check out *Business Publications Rates and Data,* and the *Standard Periodical Directory.* Either one of these directories should provide you with a comprehensive listing of magazines, journals, and newsletters in your field.

WHEN TO GET STARTED

Do you know what the Number One cause of failure is? Some experts will tell you it's under-financing, while others will claim it is poor planning. We're talking, however, about low-investment businesses, so financing should not be a problem. And proper planning is something you're learning about while reading this book.

No, the Number One factor that may cause you to fail in small business is procrastination! A business that is never started is a business that can never succeed. Because repair and maintenance businesses—and most other undertakings listed in this book—are so easy to start, you have no excuse to procrastinate. The time for daydreaming about hoped-for financial success is over. This is an "action" book, and as you continue to read please make a pledge to yourself. Pledge that on the very day that you reach the final page you will take the first steps toward setting yourself up in your own independent business. And then follow through.

Heeding the advice of the successful businesspeople you meet on these pages, learning from their mistakes and profiting from their money-making experiences, you can't help but succeed.

4

Buy a Wealth-Producing Machine

Can a machine make you rich? It depends on what you do with it, and, of course, what your goals are. This chapter is about machines that can put as much money in your bank account as you allow them to.

EARN BIG MONEY USING SPECIALIZED EQUIPMENT

How can a machine make you rich? By performing an important service for other people or other businesses—a service for which they are willing to pay well. In order for it to do this, it must be a piece of equipment that:

1. Performs a function that is useful to a good many people.
2. Is not needed frequently enough by these people to warrant their going out and buying one for themselves.

You may wonder how one machine that costs less than $1,500 to acquire can earn really big money for you. Can just one machine in that price category really do it? In many cases, yes. But in other cases where the machine merely earns you a good spare-time income of several hundred dollars a week, you don't have to be satisfied. Why? Because your early profits can pay for additional machines, run by people hired by you for the purpose.

In other words, once you develop a successful machine-based business in your community, you can repeat the process over and over again in other communities. That's one way to make really big money with an investment of under $1,500.

Another way is to acquire a more expensive machine with the same investment. How? By purchasing on time, or leasing. These methods will be explored throughout this chapter.

But for now, let's look at how one machine that costs less than $1,500 can make you a good, solid, spare-time income. Let's take a case history from my files.

DOLLARS ON WHEELS

Sid T. invested $850 in a machine that earns him an average of $250 a week for about 20 hours of work performed during the early evening and on weekends. The machine is a parking lot striper. It paints the lines that separate the parking spaces outside shopping centers, office buildings, and factories. With Sid at the controls, it automatically deposits an even coat of white paint on the macadam.

Sid gets his customers with virtually no advertising. He does have a listing in the phone book classified section, but most of his business comes from a simple and effective technique he has worked out. After leaving his regular job each day, he takes a little drive. The drive may take him to a shopping center, a factory, or a medical arts building— any location that provides parking for its employees or customers. He examines the parking lot and notes the condition of the paint stripes.

If the paint is faded, Sid contacts the owners of the property and offers to do the needed work for them.

"Sometimes I contact them by phone, most often by writing a letter, and occasionally through a personal visit," Sid reports. "In more than half of the cases, I get the assignment. Many people comment to me, 'I've been meaning to do something about that, but just haven't gotten around to it.' "

By contacting prospects who obviously need the work, by offering to do it at a reasonable price, and by simply being a johnny-on-the-spot, Sid has built a thriving business. And that business is typical of what anyone can do with a machine that performs a needed service. Sid's money-maker is a paint-striping apparatus; yours might be a tape recorder or a snowplow, but in the right hands, all of the machines listed in this chapter are money-makers.

MAKE A MONEY-MAKER MAKE MORE MONEY

Anyone can buy a machine and set himself or herself up in business. And almost anyone can make a profit doing it. But to make the really good money—to get top return on the time you plan to put in—you need to "program" your machine-based business.

Look at it this way. A machine by itself can do nothing. It must be operated or "programmed." The same with a business, especially one that is based on a machine. You could own the world's fanciest printing press, but unless you printed the right things with it, it would be little more than a gadget. That's why in this chapter we're dealing with outstanding methods that have been proven successful by spare-time entrepreneurs. They've developed unique systems that work extremely well with the machines they utilize. You're going to learn how to do the same thing.

HOW A $1,300 MACHINE MAKES A MILLION

An example of how far a machine-based business can go is provided by the experience of housewife Florence M., who needed money to help put her three children through college. With the money she's made, she could do the same for dozens of kids.

Flo's machine was a printing press. With a little imagination, she was able to "program" a thriving business based on that offset press. She got the idea one day while driving past a quick print shop, a store that can duplicate almost any document in volume in a very short period of time.

"I had read that such businesses can be learned by anyone because the presses are easy to operate," she recalls. "They are really office machines. Many offices these days have offset presses. All you do is type up a master plate, install it on the machine, and press a button."

Flo's problem was that she didn't have enough money to open a fully-equipped print shop. "One press . . . yes, I could afford the thousand dollars a used unit would cost. But a complete shop with photocopy machines, etc? No way!"

So Flo didn't open a quick print shop. What she did do worked out much better than that.

"I began trying to think of things I could produce and sell with a printing press, rather than printing work I could do for others. While having coffee at a luncheonette one afternoon my big idea struck me. I was doodling on the tablemat . . . you know, one of those that have puzzles imprinted on them. Next to me, a man was reading a newspaper. And then I got the idea."

Why not, she mused, sell diners and luncheonettes on the idea of providing their patrons with tablemats imprinted with the morning's news? While waiting for the coffee or food to arrive, patrons could get a quick summary of what has happened overnight, a capsule news summary that would appeal to just about anyone.

At first Flo thought of selling the tablemats to the eating establishments, but then she realized that for it to be profitable she'd have to charge almost as much as a full-fledged newspaper would cost—and in that case, the restaurants might just as well hand out newspapers. So she thought of something better.

FOLLOW THE LEADERS

How do the leaders in the news business—the newspapers themselves—make most of their money? By selling advertising, of course. And that's precisely what Flo did.

"Naturally, on a piece of paper the size of a tablemat you can't have large ads," she states. "So what I decided to do was to include a newsy ad 'column.' It's called *Today's Bargains*. It tells people what's on sale, and where, during the coming day. Various local businesses and even regional department and discount stores buy 'mentions' in the column. This provides my profit, and it provides readers with helpful information."

Here's how Flo set up her business:

1. She bought a used offset press for under $1000. The seller gave her a brief, but complete course on how to use it.

2. She went to a regular printshop and had it print a starting quantity of what she calls "master mats." These merely contain a masthead and a border, printed in colored ink. There is no printing inside the border. This allows Flo to type in the day's news and her *Today's Bargains* column. Actually, she types this material on a paper plate that is installed on her press, and then she runs the tablemats through the press, and out comes the latest edition of *Tablemat News*. What she has typed appears inside the pre-printed border.

3. Flo's supply of news came through an arrangement she

worked out with a local radio station. She goes to the station each evening, looks over the news it is preparing for the next morning, and makes note of the items she wants to include in *Tablemat News*. In return for this, a streamer across the bottom of *Tablemat* informs people that to be fully informed they should listen to the radio station.

4. Flo offered her "publication" free of charge to all local eating establishments that served breakfast and lunch. The only requirement was that each place use the tablemats regularly—no other tablemats allowed prior to 2:00 p.m.

"This business had me working rather unusual hours," Flo concedes, "but it was well worth it. I would go to the radio station at about 1:00 a.m., then return home and go to press an hour later. At 4:00 a.m., a part-timer I'd hired would arrive to pick up the material and deliver it to the participating diners and luncheonettes."

You may have noticed that Flo's story is told in the past tense. That's not because she has gone out of business, but simply because things have changed. Actually, "grown" would be a better word. Her enterprise was so successful in her home community that she has branched out, first to a town about 20 miles away, and then to a growing list of communities. At first, the same edition of *Tablemat News* was distributed in each of the communities, but as her territory grew she began to publish separate editions so that local news could be included.

The various editions of *Tablemat News* are now published not in her home but in a printing plant Flo has built for the purpose. Her unusual hours? They're over for her. Employees handle that now, with Flo providing 9-to-5 supervision.

A large concern recently offered Flo $1,000,000 for the business. She turned the offer down. "If it's grown that much in just a few years," she comments, "my mind boggles at the thought of how much more it can grow in the coming years. I want to stay with it."

SET YOUR PROSPERITY GOAL

One of the great things about a machine-based business is that it can be run at just about any level you desire:

- A simple, easy-to-run business that brings in extra cash amounting to one or two hundred dollars per week
- An ambitious undertaking (still part-time) in which you and the

machine work together in a "partnership" that brings in big
dollars
- An enterprise with full-time potential that allows you to expand
  as far as your aspirations take you

It's important to remember that even an inexpensive piece of
equipment—a common machine we see in use practically every day—
can be the basis of a highly profitable enterprise. This happens when the
machine performs a service needed by many people who don't require
the service quite often enough to warrant going out and buying such a
machine for themselves.

You'll see a number of examples of this in the list of money-
making machines that follows.

46 INEXPENSIVE MACHINES THAT CAN MAKE YOU RICH

Here are the machines that provide many of today's most needed
and most profitable services. The brief comments will introduce you to
the potential offered by each machine. Later we'll discuss how to pick
the right machine for you and how to get your money-maker in high
gear.

Addressing Machine: Merchants and other businessmen
know the importance of directing their direct mail advertising to
people rather than box numbers or "occupants." That's why they
frequently use the facilities of local addressing services. With an
addressing machine and a file of names and addresses compiled
from local phone books, you can provide a valuable and profitable service.

Auto Diagnosis: With an electronic automobile analyzer
costing about $500, you can be of great service to people who are
shopping for used cars. They call on you to check out the condition of a vehicle they're interested in buying, and you connect
your machine and give them an informed analysis.

Auto Painting: Used car lots, taxi firms, and other companies
that have fleets of cars are prime prospects for an auto painting
service that you can establish with the aid of spraying equipment
and a clean garage.

Bill Collection: Most bill collecting companies do most of
their work through the mail. Rather than send out form letters,
you can dispatch personal-appearing letters addressed to the individual debtors by using a relatively inexpensive mini-computer

and printing terminal. The equipment can be purchased or obtained on a lease basis. See the example given later in this chapter.

Bus Trips: Organized bus trips to such places as the theater, the beach, amusement parks, and sightseeing areas can make good money for you. In this case, your "machine" is a used bus that you purchase with a $1,500 down payment, or a more expensive vehicle obtained on a lease basis.

Camera Project: There are many ways that such an everyday item as a camera can make excellent money for you. Some of them are discussed in detail in Chapter 10.

Canvas Covers: With a sewing machine installed in a utility trailer or aboard a van, you can custom-fit canvas covers for boats and awnings for recreational vehicles. In the Northeast, Denis M. goes from marina to marina during the summer months soliciting and obtaining assignments to install bimini tops, bridge covers, and cockpit coverings. He uses an old parcel delivery truck that he obtained "for a song."

Cassette Courses: Many businesspeople and others who don't have the time to do all the reading required to keep their knowledge up to date depend on cassette tapes. They listen to instructive or informative recordings while they drive, or even while they dress or shave. If you can get the information they need, you're in business. Put it on tape and then use several inexpensive cassette recorders to dub copies. Most cassette courses and cassette "newsletters" are sold through the mail. See Chapter 6.

Cassette Dictation: Professional people who don't require full-time secretaries often use commercial secretarial services to do their typing for them. So do traveling businessmen. You can make it easier for them by taking dictation over the phone—and you don't need to know shorthand. All you need is a cassette recorder and a $2 connector that records what comes in over the phone. The clients dictate at full speed and you do the typing at your convenience.

Cassette Tours: See the example given later in this chapter.

Cheap Car Rentals: The large car rental companies make a big deal of (and charge big money for) featuring spanking new cars that contain nary a dent or rust spot. By buying up some "cheapie" older cars, you can offer bargain rates in the car rental business. A number of cheap car rental services throughout the U.S. are earning sizable profits with such money-savers.

Computer Advertising: Painted signs are not exactly passé, but flashing-light signs are becoming more and more popular. These are small versions of what you may have seen on the sports stadium scoreboard, or atop that tall building in Times Square. You can buy a demonstrator model for under $1,500. Lease it to a bank or store, and the client types in his own sales message on a keyboard. Other business establishments will soon want to jump on the bandwagon. Check the "Franchise Opportunities" section of a large metro newspaper or a business publication for ads offering these machines.

Conference Cassettes: Many people who would like to attend business conferences and seminars but can't because of prior engagements are prospects for cassette recordings of the proceedings. If you live in or near a city where such events are frequently held, you can obtain the cassette "rights" to the speeches and discussions. Record what goes on and then use a rented mailing list to offer the tapes to the prospects. Hannah J. does this and clears $17,000 a year in her spare time. She uses the same mailing lists that the seminar sponsors used in announcing their seminars. Many of the people who failed to sign up for a seminar do sign up for the tapes. She gives the seminar sponsors a 20% royalty.

Custom Developing: Most photo-finishing is done these days by computer-controlled machines. That's fine for the average run-of-the-mill snapshot, but serious photographers require something more. And not all serious photographers are interested in developing their own work. Those are the people who patronize custom developing firms. With a quality enlarger and related darkroom equipment, you can accommodate such people.

Driver Training: In this case your machine is an automobile equipped with dual controls. You'll need a special license and some other regulations will have to be met, but driver training is a comparatively easy service to provide, and it's a profitable business.

Dry Cleaning: In this case, the machine is not yours and it's not even used by you. Instead, you locate a volume dry cleaner who is willing to handle your work for you. Your customers are people who live in large apartment complexes. You provide pickup and delivery dry cleaning service. Because of the efficiency involved in dealing with a large number of customers who live close to each other, you can make a profitable enterprise out of this. Opportunities exist in virtually every sizable community.

Floor Polisher: Refer back to Chapter 3 and you'll be reminded of the profits that can be earned in this machine-based business.

Heavy Construction Equipment: Grading equipment, front end loaders, backhoes, etc. all perform important tasks and their owner-operators earn top money when they contract their services. In this case, since we're limiting your investment to $1,500, you are not really an owner-operator, you are a lessee-operator. The equipment you use in your business is leased, not purchased outright. Details on leasing come later in the chapter.

Helium-Filled Balloons: It's been described as one of the most profitable "little" business opportunities in America, and that it is. The reason is that it is a rare parent who would deny a young child's eager desire for such a balloon when offered by a vendor on a street corner, at an amusement area, in a shopping center, or wherever else families congregate. The equipment can be obtained inexpensively, and the profit margin on these fast-selling items is tremendous.

Home Insulation: With an inexpensive cellulose-blowing machine and some bags of cellulose, you can be in business installing insulation in the homes of people who want to conserve energy. Write to the National Cellulose Insulation Manufacturers Association, 220 Seegers Ave., Elk Grove Village, IL 60007, for details on how to get into this lucrative service field.

Income Tax Preparation: Yes, this can be a machine-based business, thanks to what is known as a programmable calculator. For considerably less than $500 you can buy a Texas Instruments programmable which comes complete with a book telling you all about how to program it and how to use the little printer that you buy with it. You program it to handle the data required for the current year's short form tax returns, set yourself up in a storefront or shopping mall lobby during the tax season, and you're in business. People give you their figures, you enter them on the calculator, and out comes an adding machine-like tape printed with the figures to be entered on the tax return.

Industrial Laundry: With a few used washing machines installed in your basement or garage, you can provide a needed service for gas stations, small factories, restaurants, and the like. What you do is clean the work clothes their employees wear, making pickups and deliveries once or twice a week.

Key Duplication: You've seen key duplicating machines in stores, shopping center lobbies, and elsewhere. A heavy-trafficked area where you have not seen such machines is a potential money-making location for you. No advertising or promotion is needed. All you do is buy the machine, get some practice, and pay the rent.

Lawn Mower Sharpening: It's a spring and summer business, but one that allows you to really make hay while the sun shines. Then relax with the profits during the fall and winter.

Limo Service: You in a chauffeur's uniform? Why not? You can make a lot more money than the liveried class ever made if you provide the limousine that goes along with your uniform. Your customers are people who want to be driven to weddings, funerals, other social gatherings, or even just on shopping trips. And, yes, you can latch on to a limo for less than $1,500 . . . down. It can be several years old as long as it's maintained in immaculate condition.

Lunch Wagon: The key to success here is going to where the people are and the restaurants aren't. Construction jobs, wilderness recreation areas, and sporting events are all prime locations.

Mall Entertainment Machines: People are fascinated by biorhythms, horoscopes, and computer photographs. These "printouts" can be handled by electronic computer-like devices that can be purchased for under $1,500. Set yourself up at shopping malls, country fairs, or flea markets, and you'll have an excellent money-maker.

Mimeograph Machine: People go to quick print shops when they need hundreds or thousands of copies, but when only a few dozen or a hundred are needed, they save money by having the work mimeographed instead of printed. Their desire to save money is your chance to make money, and you can do it with an electric mimeo that can be bought for about $250. Do the work at home, of course, in order to save on overhead. Contact restaurants, offices, professional people, and political organizations. You can handle their menus, order forms, contract forms, and ballyhoo sheets.

Motel Laundry Service: Start with a few used washing machines and you can be handling the linen cleaning work for many of the motels in your area. Pickup and delivery is on a daily basis, but it can be accomplished at "odd" hours worked in and around your regular job.

Motor Home or Camper Rental: It seems wasteful for people to own motor homes and campers that they use for only two or three weeks of the year. That's why many families rent rather than buy. You can start with one secondhand unit purchased with less than $1,500 down, and expand out of profits.

News Tablemat: Need I say more? You've already read about the spectacular success of Florence M.

PA System Rentals: Many organizations, some businesses, and even a few individuals have need for PA systems from time to time. There's money to be made by renting such equipment to them. For well under $1,500 you can buy several units, making multiple rentals each day.

Parking Lot Striper: Sid T.'s story is told earlier in this chapter. Perhaps you can repeat his success.

Portable Disco System: This is a business in which you rent out your DJ talents along with your portable record-playing equipment. With the latest dance music, a good line of patter, and high quality equipment you can be earning good money providing entertainment at parties, in local nightclubs, and at fund-raising events.

Rug Cleaning: A number of companies offering rug cleaning equipment advertise regularly in the business opportunity magazines. They also provide the needed training.

Sailboat Charters: Under a low down payment, extended payment plan, you can take title to a sailboat that will not only be fun for you to use, but profitable to charter to others. Many sailboat purchasers charter out their crafts to meet their monthly payments. The smarter ones realize they can actually make a profit at it. They do this by using the boat less themselves, freeing it for rentals more weeks and weekends during the year.

Snowplow: A four-wheel-drive vehicle equipped with a snowplow can have you earning a good winter-month income. Even if you have a regular 9-to-5 job you can profit in this business, because most plowing has to be done prior to the start of the business day so that people can get to work and drive into business locations.

Swimming Pool Maintenance: Armed with vacuum equipment and the other inexpensive appliances that are required, you can set up a pool-cleaning business, with the actual work performed by you or by teenagers you hire.

T-Shirt Decal Transfer Machine: With equipment that costs several hundred dollars or even less, you are in one of today's "hottest" businesses. You can work from home, serving the needs of amateur athletic teams and recreational clubs, or you can set up a booth in the nearest shopping mall.

Telephone Answering Service: Many people are turned off by recorded answering devices. That's why a lot of professional people still turn to answering services staffed by real live people. The needed equipment can be leased from the phone company and set up in your home. The only drawback is that somebody has to be there most or all of the time—unless the arrangement you make with your clients is for specific hours only.

Telephone Info Service: Automatic telephone answering devices can be money-makers when you use them to provide weather forecasts, brief news summaries, local sports scores or other needed information. People call for whatever information you're offering, and are greeted by a commercial announcement that comes prior to the information they seek. Your money is made by selling the "commercials" to local business establishments. More on this in Chapter 8.

Tent Rentals: Many outdoor events are held under tents, and most organizations sponsoring such events rent the tents they need. By providing the tent and guidance in putting it up, you have a business that can bring in a hundred or even several hundred dollars a week, depending on the number and the size of the tents you offer.

Upholstery Cleaning: This works very much like the rug cleaning service listed earlier.

Vending Machines: If you can distinguish the "sharpie" firms that merely want to sell you a nearly useless machine from the legitimate companies that have genuinely profitable vending devices available, you can establish an easy-to-service route of coin-operated money-makers. Check the "Business Opportunity" ads in your paper and in appropriate magazines.

Voice Stress Analyzer: A growing number of companies recognize the value of the voice stress analyzing machine during job interviews as a means of choosing top-notch employees. One such machine can be bought for about $1,500. With that device and a bit of practice, you can be providing a valuable service.

Word Processing: Home typing has always been an attractive means of making money. Now you can make even more money at it by means of automation. Automatic typewriters are becoming more and more common, and they allow you to turn out more work. Naturally, you still have to sit at a keyboard, but errors are corrected much more rapidly, and when the same letter is being sent to a number of different people on your client's list, you only have to type the letter once. Such machines can be leased at a surprisingly low monthly rate.

HOW TO PICK THE RIGHT MONEY-MAKING MACHINE FOR YOU

Because most businesses based on the use of machines involve services, you make your selection of a business in much the same manner as suggested for repairs and maintenance businesses in Chapter 3.

There is, however, one thing to bear in mind. You need not be limited to a machine that costs under $1,500. You can obtain a much more valuable piece of equipment and still set yourself up in business for less than the $1,500 maximum established for the businesses listed in this book.

You've seen, in the listing of businesses above, the two ways that you can gain access to really expensive equipment:

1. Leasing the machine on a monthly fee basis
2. Purchasing it on time

If you plan to purchase the equipment on time, it is usually best to start out by leasing it, if possible, because this allows you to "test" your business before making a firm financial commitment. During the test period you can determine if the amount of business you obtain lives up to your expectations, and you can also find out if the equipment you have leased is precisely right for the job.

Picking the right money-making equipment for you, then, depends on these factors:

1. The need for the service that the equipment provides
2. Your ability to operate the equipment
3. The equipment's cost, or its availability under a lease plan

Now let's look at some equipment-based businesses in action.

GUIDE TO PROVIDING A MACHINE-BASED SERVICE

When you build a spare-time business around a machine, you usually do one of two things:

1. You install the machine in your home or apartment and provide the service from that location
2. You use a portable piece of equipment that is operated at some remote location

With 46 machine-based businesses listed in this chapter, it would be impossible for me to give full particulars on how to start and operate each of them. But since all of them fall into one of the above two categories, I can show you how people have achieved outstanding success in each of the categories. Then you can adapt what they did to the particular machine you pick for your own undertaking.

MAKE MONEY WITH A HOME-BASED MACHINE

One of the nicest advantages of having a home-based machine to help you run a profitable sideline is that you can generally run your machine during whatever hours you feel like working, not just when it's convenient for the customer. When you receive an assignment, you agree to have the work done by a certain time, but it doesn't matter what hours you choose for actually doing it.

Thus you can turn on your bill collection machine, mimeograph, T-shirt decal transfer machine, or automatic washers right after breakfast on Saturday morning, at 1:00 a.m. any weekday morning, at 6:00 in the evening . . . or whenever is most convenient.

This brings us to our first rule for running your home-based enterprise:

Discipline yourself to set a regular schedule despite the flexible hours.

Pick the time of day or the day of the week that is most agreeable to you, but then make that a regular work period that is almost never violated. Otherwise your output will diminish, schedules won't be met, and customers will be disappointed.

Tom R. uses a leased word processing machine to run a bill collecting service. Business firms and professional people in his community turn delinquent accounts over to him and he endeavors to make collections. When he succeeds, he gets to keep 40% of the amount collected.

Tom never goes banging on doors, nor does he make phone calls to the people who owe money. What he does is send out a series of letters, all typed automatically by his word processor. He sets two hours aside each evening after supper for this. The letters are dropped in the mail on his way to work the next morning.

"It's an easy schedule," he reports, "so easy, in fact, that at first I was tempted to skip an evening or two thinking I could make up the work the next night. But I soon found that if you want to build a highly profitable business, you've got to stick to a regular routine."

The only "outside" work Tom does (other than dropping off the mail in the morning) is to make occasional visits to his clients' offices to pick up the delinquent account lists. Everything else is done at home. And this leads us to the second rule for conducting a business at home:

Make sure your business does not violate local zoning regulations.

If your home happens to be in a commercial area, there should be no problem. But if, as in Tom's case, you live in a residential zone, then you should be sure that there is no flow of commercial traffic to and from your home, and that any sign you may have hanging out front meets local requirements. Check your municipal hall for details.

You may wonder why business and professional people turn to Tom for bill collecting when they could type the dunning letters themselves. Yes, they could do that—but at considerable expense. Tom's "standard" letters are not really standard. Each starts out with the name and address of the recipient, the greeting contains the recipient's name, and the body of each letter also makes use of the name once or twice.

"It's the personal angle that makes them effective," he reports. "The letters are typed on my clients' own letterheads, just as if it came directly from their own offices. It would take too much of a secretary's time to type a series of letters to each delinquent account individually. Printed form letters are not as effective as personal ones. Thus, because I can do the work quickly and at less cost than his own office can, the client turns to me."

And that brings us to the third rule:

In order for you to make a profit, your service must be cheaper, faster, or better than what the customer could do for himself.

Tom meets this requirement because of the automatic nature of his leased typing machine. The basic text of each of the letters he sends out is already entered in the "memory" of the typewriter. All he has to do is type in the name and address of the recipient and push a button. The machine does the rest, producing a neat, professional-looking letter. He can turn out hundreds of letters each evening, and not one of them contains an error.

"O.K.," you say, "that takes care of faster and better, but how about cheaper? Doesn't the machine cost Tom a lot of money?"

Not at all when you compare it to his income. He leases the word processor for about $200 a month. His gross collections per month average out to about $3,000. Here's a breakdown of the figures:

Collections	$3,000
	x .40
Commission	1200
Total Overhead	- 300
Net Profit	$900

Tom devotes a maximum of three hours each day to his business: two hours in the evening processing the letters and one hour during the day mailing the letters and picking up new lists from clients. This gives him an hourly rate of pay amounting to $13.85.

"That's pretty good for a business that I run from the comfort of my home," Tom comments. "And it's getting better. I'm soon going to add another word processing machine to double my output."

MAKE MONEY WITH PORTABLE EQUIPMENT

You'll see from the list of machine-based businesses that many involve equipment operated away from your home. In some cases you are the operator; in others the equipment is used by other people. Bill A. has developed a unique business in the latter category. His equipment is cassette recorders.

Bill has refined his enterprise to the point where most of the work is actually conducted by other people. All he does is make collections and check to see that the recorders are kept working. Thus he is heeding the first rule involved in an away-from-home business centering on equipment:

Have as much of the work as possible done by the machine and/or the customer, minimizing the amount of time you must put in.

Not all enterprises lend themselves to this rule equally well, but in Bill's case, once the preliminary work was done the business became almost automatic in nature. Bill lives in an important American tourist city. He rents his cassette machines, along with pre-recorded tapes, to the tourists. The tapes provide a continuing commentary and guide to the city. He offers "walking tour" versions and "driving tour" versions.

The tourist is instructed where to begin the tour. At that location he or she turns on the cassette and is provided with a description of the history and significance of the immediate area. Then the tourist is told where to go next and how to get there, at which time the commentary continues.

The preliminary work involved in setting up Bill's business consisted mainly of writing the commentary and hiring a local radio announcer to record it. Then Bill bought several dozen cassette machines on time and dubbed the original tape so that each of the machines would have a copy of its own.

The next step was to arrange to have local gift shops serve as rental agencies. For this service, they get to keep 15% of the $7.50 rental fee. This brings us to Rule Number Two:

Make your service as easy as possible for your customers to obtain and use.

Your machine can perform one of the most valuable services in the world, but unless it is readily available to the people for whom it is intended, it can't make much money for you. There would be few customers, for example, if Bill required them to go to his apartment in order to rent the tapes. That's why so many rental operations are conducted out of existing stores on a commission basis.

Bill's success in his home city has led him to launch a similar project in another city located some 50 miles away. And thus we arrive at the third rule:

Duplicate your success until you achieve your financial goals.

When your business is based on portable equipment operated away from your home, it's a lot easier to make a carbon copy of your initial enterprise, and duplicate the income as well. To expand a home-based business, you generally have to move the undertaking out of your home into a commercial location. It's the type of business that needs a headquarters, and the larger you get the bigger the headquarters you will need.

On the other hand, when you use portable equipment close to where the customer is, all you have to do is place additional equipment near where another group of potential customers is located.

There is every reason to expect that a business which is successful in one community will be equally profitable in many other cities. That's why there's not just one McDonald's Restaurant, why there are many

Holiday Inns, and why Sears has stores all over the country and in other countries as well.

You may not wish to become a multi-city millionaire, but it's good to know that if you can make money here, you can also make money there. Opportunities for expansion are as good today as they ever were. And you have a distinct advantage over most of the people whose stories are told in this book. They learned from trial and error, and in so doing they paved the way for you to read about and then duplicate their success.

5

Profit from the Work of Others

Although you can build a hefty spare-time income working alone, why limit yourself to what you can produce by yourself? Regardless of the type of business you launch, it often makes sense to increase your productive capacity by enlisting the work of others.

Think of today's dynasties that began with one person working alone—Henry Ford building his motorcar, Margaret Rudkin baking bread at her Pepperidge Farm, Richard Sears shipping watches through the mail—and you'll realize that while these business empires were launched with the ideas of one person, they grew because of the work of many people.

And if it makes sense to expand a business with the labor of other people, it can make even more sense to start out that way. This chapter tells how you can put other people to work earning money for you right from the start.

KEEP A SLICE OF EVERYBODY ELSE'S PAYCHECK

The 50 businesses you'll learn about in this chapter are all based on one theme: services performed by others. They do the work, you coordinate it, and everyone benefits. And the more people involved in your plan, the more you make. That's because you get to keep a percentage of what each person receives for each hour worked.

Here, in a nutshell, is the plan:

1. You pick the type of service you wish to offer.
2. By running "Help Wanted" ads, you obtain a list of people willing to work part-time in that field.
3. You advertise the availability of your service and then put the people on your list to work performing the assignments you receive.
4. The customer pays you, you deduct your cut, and your workers are paid out of the balance.

What type of service can your business offer? It can be as simple as doing odd jobs for homeowners or as complex as putting up buildings. The principle is the same in each case. What you are doing in most cases is serving as a contractor who sub-contracts the work. This way you stand to make big money for very little individual effort on your part. And because your business is based on a service rather than a product line, only a small investment is required.

HOW $1,000 STARTS A BIG-PROFIT PERSONNEL AGENCY

Like David L., you will pick a field that you are comfortable with —probably in line with your own previous work experience. David is a retired office manager, and providing temporary office personnel was the field he chose.

"There are a number of franchises in this field," David comments, "but none of them was operating in my town. At first I looked into buying such a franchise, but the fee of $20,000 turned me off. I realized that I could start an agency by myself at far less cost."

The "far less cost" amounted to $1,000. David ran an inexpensive ad in the local newspaper that read something like this:

> Typists, receptionists, clerical workers, keypunch operators, other office personnel needed for temporary work. Call Riverview Office Temporaries at 000-0000.

"Even I was surprised at the response I got from that ad," David reports. "But I should have known that there are a lot of people out there looking for 'occasional' work—people who don't want to work all the time but who are eager to take jobs that last a few days or a few weeks."

As soon as he'd compiled a list of workers in various office categories, David ran another ad, this one in the "Business Services" column of his newspaper's classified section:

Need temporary office help? We have skilled people ready to go to work for you by the day, the
week, or for longer periods. Call Riverview Office
Temporaries at 000-0000.

"I also sent small printed notices to many business firms in the
area, " David notes. "Again, the response surprised me. Obviously, I
had found an important local need, and by offering to fill it, I was
finding many takers."

Why do so many business firms seek temporary help? Other than
to have personnel to fill in during vacation periods and other times of
staff shortage, they want to avoid the bother and expense of having to
pay employee benefits such as retirement and hospitalization. Also,
many firms have varying workloads. Work may be heavy at one time of
the year and light at another, so rather than maintain a full payroll
when the personnel are not really needed, they call in temporaries. An
accounting office, for example, would have a heavy workload in the
spring prior to the income tax deadline and a lighter workload after
that.

Thus there is a need for companies such as David's. His slice of the
payroll? He keeps one fourth of the money charged a client for the temporary personnel it has requested. If the client is charged $6.00 an hour,
David's firm keeps $1.50 of that and $4.50 goes to the worker.

You may wonder why workers are willing to give up such a hefty
slice of their pay. David explains: "It's for the privilege of being able to
work when they want to and not work when they don't want to. If
Company A needs a typist for three weeks, I go down my list. If Typist
Number 1 doesn't feel like working just then, I give a call to Typist
Number 2, and so forth. It's an arrangement where everybody wins."

Especially David. He wins to the tune of $650 net profit per week.
Admittedly, he spends a lot of time on the telephone, but the business is
run from the comfort of his home. He has an answering service take
calls while he's away, so he's free to go out and play golf and enjoy other
retirement pursuits once the day's assignments are taken care of.

"Why the $1,000 investment," you inquire, "if the business was
started with two inexpensive newspaper ads?" Of course there were
small expenses for supplies, a business phone and the like—but the
main part of the investment was set aside for initial payrolls. That's
because although the companies are billed on a monthly basis, David's
workers are paid each week for whatever work they put in.

"I had to have a cushion to carry me over until the money started
coming in," David notes. "Admittedly, $1,000 wasn't much, so I
started small and expanded my payroll 'cushion' out of profits."

USE PEOPLE LEVERAGE TO BUILD A BUSINESS

"People leverage" is much like financial leverage. With money, you use a few of your own dollars to gain the benefit of many dollars provided by somebody else. An example is when you buy a car or a home. Your down payment gives you the use of that vehicle or building. In business, financial leverage allows you to earn profits on a total investment, when you have actually put up only a small percentage of the investment.

The same is true with people leverage. You may work only 15-20 hours a week, but since you have many other people putting in a lot of hours as well, you're "leveraging" your own work so that it brings in money from the work of all the other people involved in your project.

Providing temporary help is not the only way it's done. In some of the businesses listed in this chapter, the people actually work for you instead of for a client. They enable you to provide a service you could never tackle alone, and thus to earn much more money than you could ever earn alone.

50 "PEOPLE" BUSINESSES NEEDED ALMOST EVERYWHERE

So now we come to the high-profit businesses that you can run alone by assigning the work to others. Although you'll probably want to choose a line of work with which you are already familiar, be aware of the fact that it's possible to pick a field where your workers know a lot more about the work than you do. This is especially true when your business offers the service of experts in a given field. You might not be an expert—but you know how to get them for people who need them, and you're paid well for doing it.

Here are the 50 "people" opportunities I suggest you consider. Later, we'll discuss how to pick the right field for you and how to get it started.

Appraisals: It's easy to find someone who can appraise a piece of real estate—but what happens when a person or a business firm needs an appraisal of a piece of art, a boat, a vehicle, some machinery, an old manuscript, an antique, household items, a specialized business, etc? You can fill these needs by assembling a list of local experts in various fields to be on call for appraisal assignments, and you get to keep 20% of the fee.

Automobile Transport: People who plan to travel long distances for an extended stay often want their cars with them when they get there but don't want the hassle of driving the long distance. By running classified ads, you locate other people who are looking for free transportation to the same areas. They get to drive the car for free and you get to collect a fee from the owner.

Baby Sitters: Some young couples are lucky enough to have a favorite baby sitter available whenever they call; others have to search. By setting up a registry of baby sitters in your community you can provide a needed service to sitters seeking work and parents seeking sitters.

Bartenders: Many bartending jobs are part-time positions. Many bars are left at practically the last minute without someone to pour the drinks. Compile a list of persons who want to do this type of work, note the days and hours they are available, and drinking establishments will look to you first when the need arises.

Bartering Service: Suppose there were 100 people each working for several hours a week on special projects, and you were given $1.00 for each hour they worked. It's been done, and you can do it, too, by setting up a bartering service. This is an arrangement in which people trade skills. Joe Smith may be good at auto mechanics and is willing to work on someone's car in exchange for someone to help him with his wallpapering. It's usually not a direct exchange. Smith may do Johnson's auto work, while Anderson helps Smith with his wallpaper project. Each person gets a time credit in the barter bank that you maintain as operator of the project. If Smith works a total of ten hours in a given period, then he's entitled to a total of ten hours work from someone else listed in the bank. How is the money earned? For your service in keeping records and getting the people together, you collect $1.00 per hour. The money is paid by the person who requested the help.

Bookkeeping Service: A lot of people with professional bookkeeping experience are looking for part-time work that they can handle largely at home. And many small businesses need part-time bookkeeping services. You can develop a profitable enterprise by signing up the businesses that need such work and then assigning the work to the bookkeepers on your list.

Business Consultants: The modern business world is highly specialized, and when businesses need advice on improving their operations, they have to turn to specialists in the field. If you live in or near a metropolitan area, it will be relatively easy for you to assemble a list of specialists in various fields who are willing to take on consulting assignments. They can be paid $50 or more per hour, and you can keep at least 10% of that.

Business Service Coordinator: There are slack periods in nearly every business, periods when people or equipment are nearly idle. That's when the owners of such firms are willing to barter their services in exchange for services from some other company. Thus, a radio station might run commercials for a cruise line in exchange for a cruise for the owner's family; or a printing firm might exchange some of its work for free meals at a local restaurant. Where do you fit in? You sign up the companies that are willing to barter and you collect a percentage of the value of the services that are exchanged.

Car Pool Registry: With the high price of gasoline, a growing number of commuters would like to share the cost with others. To find people who go to and from the same place at the same time can be difficult. That's why they are usually willing to pay a fee to a service firm that can set up a four-person car pool. You have to live near a major metropolis to make this profitable, but if you do and if you set up a good cross-reference system, you can earn a sizable spare-time income providing a needed and even "patriotic" service.

Car Waxing: Car waxing is not a lost art; it's merely something that's difficult to arrange because you usually have to drop your car off somewhere. Enlist some young men and women who want to earn extra money by waxing cars in the owners' driveways, run some small newspaper ads, and you've got yourself a service business that should go over in just about any community.

Carpenter Service: Carpenters who want to moonlight can get all the work they desire by signing up with your service firm. Homeowners who need light carpentry can get it done with no hassle by contacting you. Everyone benefits.

Catering: A catered affair requires the talents of many people. Assemble the people and the foodstuffs, and you can provide a valuable service to families and business organizations in your area.

Clerical Service: This differs from the service you read about earlier as performed by David L., in that most of this kind of work is done in the homes of the workers rather than in the client's office. It involves dictation and typing, sending out bills, addressing envelopes, etc. It's easy to find people who are anxious to do this type of work at home, and just as easy to find small businesses that need such help.

Clipping Service: We live in a public relations-conscious society; business firms are very concerned about their image and they want to know what is said about them in the press. A profitable service business is the type that provides these companies with clippings of their press "mentions."How do they get the clippings? From companies like the one you might set up. How do you get the clippings? By running small classified ads in national magazines and offering to pay people in various cities to read their newspapers with scissors in hand. Periodically, you send your workers a list of the specific information your clients are seeking. The workers get a small fee for each item that is clipped and mailed to you.

Computer Programming: The sharp drop in the prices of microcomputers has made them available to small companies that could never afford them before. But once they get these handy machines, the business owners usually don't know the first thing about programming them. In most communities there are a number of people, amateurs and professionals alike, who are capable of handling such programming tasks. Locate them through ads and through notices sent to amateur computer clubs and you've got the basis for a profitable service.

Construction or Alteration Contractor: Most construction projects require the work of contractors in several fields ranging from masonry to carpentry, plumbing, and electrical work. What you do here is take the contract for the entire job and then subcontract the various phases of the work to skilled people and firms in the field. You have to be knowledgeable about bidding, materials, and scheduling, but if you've had experience and use good judgment you may have a highly lucrative spare-time business going for you.

Courier Service: Despite the continuing legal battle over whether private firms are allowed to compete with the U.S. Postal Service, many cities are served by private "courier" firms that deliver enveloped materials on behalf of business establishments within the same city. Retired people, students, and other part-timers serve as the couriers and you serve as the money-making coordinator of it all.

Dog Walking: This only works in large cities where most people live in apartments, but when such is the case, you can sign up older teenagers and college students to earn extra money walking dogs owned by apartment dwellers. This is being done in a number of major metropolises, and if it's not already being done in your city, opportunity beckons.

Entertainers: Musicians, singers, magicians, clowns, ventriloquists, mind-readers, and other semi-professional entertainers are constantly looking for new outlets. Owners of local nightclubs, party-givers, organizations, and shopping center operators need such talent. You'll have no trouble signing up capable entertainers, and with a large list available you should be able to fill the needs of the businesses and organizations who seek their services.

Escort Service: Accompanying members of the opposite sex to social and business functions is a pleasant way to earn extra money, and that's why escort services in medium to large sized cities have little difficulty signing up escorts. Customers are solicited through ads in the yellow pages and in regional guide publications.

Fix Anything Service: In any community there are wide-ranging "fix-it" talents in the population. Create a register of individuals who are willing to do spare-time repair work, list the type of work they do, and you'll be able to find the right person to do almost any job that is assigned to you. Then advertise that you can fix just about anything. Each time you get a call, check your register for the proper person to assign, and you've got yourself a welcome commission.

Floor Waxing: You saw a profitable example of this in Chapter 3. In that example, Kevin C. began by doing the work himself. It's not necessary to start that way. You can have others do the physical labor right from the start.

Foreign Language Translations: All companies that do business overseas have need for translations, and many don't have linguists on their staffs. That's where you can come in, once you have assembled a list of people with native tongues representing the major languages of the world.

Fund-Raising Coordinator: Leaders of many organizations and charity drives have come to realize that in order to raise funds effectively they need professionals to steer the campaign. You can become that professional, especially if you've had experience in similar work on a volunteer basis. You serve as coordinator of the organization's own volunteers who do most of the actual soliciting.

Guided Tours: If your area is frequented by tourists and if it has a number of nearby sightseeing attractions, you can make money by signing up local residents to provide tours of the area. The guides who work for you can use their own cars (for family groups) or mini-buses (for larger numbers of people).

Handbill Delivery: Even though a number of what used to be known as handbills are now distributed as inserts in daily newspapers, business firms that don't want to be "buried" with a lot of other advertising still prefer to have their flyers distributed by hand. Enlist the hands of a number of youngsters to do the work, and you can be of profitable service to such firms.

Health Care Personnel: There's a growing emphasis on in-home care of convalescents. You can capitalize on this by serving as a clearing-house for people who seek nurses, physical therapists, and other health care workers.

Home Hair Care: Convalescents require hair-styling just as much as those who can get out and around. Many people skilled at this work are willing to take on assignments in the homes of clients. If you live in or near an affluent neighborhood, you can also find clients among the rich, people who can afford to have groomers come to them.

House Cleaning: You set up teams of fast-working home cleaners who perform their tasks efficiently and well. Any woman who's ever despaired of the difficulty of getting a "cleaning woman" is a hot prospect for your service.

Income Tax Preparation: This is a seasonal business in which a heavy workload develops during the first four months of the year. Many people are fully capable of compiling income tax returns but don't want to go to the bother of seeking clients. You bring the number-crunchers and the taxpayers together and you'll receive a slice of everybody's income.

Instruction: Chapter 7 tells all about this fascinating field. I also list it here because most instruction-type businesses are based on the use of other people's work. You sign up the teachers and then enroll the students, keeping the difference between what the students pay and what the teachers receive.

Laborers: They load trucks, they move heavy objects, they help at construction projects, they cut brush and trees, they move dirt and rocks—and they make money for you. When companies have uneven workloads (periods of little work followed by periods of a lot of work), the most practical thing for them to do is to hire temporary workers. Your profitable specialty is to provide those workers.

Mass Production Art: The market for "art" has never been greater, even when it is the type of painting that is turned out on a mass-production basis by people willing and able to do that type of work. A single painting takes an artist a lot more time than if he or she were to repeat the same piece of work over and over again, making many almost-duplicate paintings. Yet each can be sold as genuine and original paintings. Get people to do this work and then sell it to gift shops, department stores, restaurants, and offices and you've got yourself a real money-maker.

Minority Employment Service: Most progressive firms pride themselves these days on being Equal Opportunity Employers, and even many firms that are not willingly progressive are required by federal regulations to have members of minority groups adequately represented on their staffs. It is often costly for such firms to seek out the minority group people they need. You can be of service to them, as well as to minority group members who are seeking good jobs, by serving as a clearing house. Your money comes from the employer, not from the job applicant.

Newspaper Delivery: Newspaper delivery routes remain a profitable sideline because it's easy to find car owners who are willing to make deliveries during the early morning hours or late afternoon hours when they are not working at their regular jobs. While most daily and Sunday newspapers maintain their own company-operated routes in their immediate coverage areas, they won't deliver anything but their own publications. Independent services deliver all papers that are available locally, and they function best in areas outside the delivery area of the local daily.

Odd Jobs: High school kids and college students welcome the work and homeowners seek the help. You can be of service to both categories by bringing them together.

Office Cleaning: This is almost always after-hours work. The cleaners go in when the office is closed. This makes it easy for you to enlist workers, because it doesn't conflict with their regular employment.

Office Personnel: You've read about the profitable experience of David L. earlier in this chapter. With the proper background, and in the right community, you can duplicate his success.

Packaged Tour Broker: Packaged tours of foreign lands are offered by many companies. Your function is to assemble groups of 30 to 40 people to go on these tours. All the work is done for you except for assembling the people. You get a commission for each tour you sell—or, occasionally, you might like to go on the tour yourself, in which case you travel free. How can you learn about such packages? Examine the ads—especially the classifieds—in the travel magazines. Also, go to your nearest travel agent and ask for brochures on a number of tours. Write to the smaller, lesser known companies that package such tours and offer your services.

Painters: House painting is a lucrative business, and it's even more so when you can paint six or ten houses at once. How can you do this? By having other people do the work for you. Why are house painters willing to give you a cut of their pay? Because you commission work for them on their days off or during slack periods, and also because they can work or not work as the mood fits them; you have enough other people on your list to fill in when the need arises.

Parcel Delivery: It's agreed that you're not going to be able to put United Parcel Service out of business. In fact, in most cases you won't even be competing with it. What you are doing is delivering packages within one relatively small area, such as a city or a county. You start out by enlisting people with station wagons or van type trucks. As your business grows you may want to develop your own delivery fleet.

Sales Personnel: More money has probably been made in the sales field than in any other line of work. Commissions are high— so high, in fact, that by assembling a group of salesmen, there's more than enough for you to take a sizable cut. See Chapter 8.

Security Guards: Everyone is becoming more security-conscious these days, and the demand for security guards to protect business establishments, factories, and private estates was never greater. The availability of workers is no problem; the work is usually part-time and it's almost always easy.

Seminars: Business firms spend hundreds of dollars per employee to see that their staff members are kept abreast of the latest developments in their field. Seminars providing such information are inexpensive to run. Your role is hiring the hall, retaining some knowledgeable speakers, and collecting the money. Chapter 7 tells all.

Share-an-Expert Service: This is something like the bartering service for homeowners that you read about earlier, only in this case the service is for business firms instead of individuals. Businessman A needs advice on buying a small computer system (he doesn't want to be over-sold by an eager salesman); Businesswoman B needs some help in choosing the right location for her new store; Businessman C wants to get guidance on making overseas sales. You barter the expertise of these various people and get a fee for doing it.

Speakers Bureau: There are loads of people who enjoy giving talks on subjects that they know well, and there are many organizations that need interesting speakers for their meetings and conventions. Bringing the two together can be your source of excellent spare-time income.

Technical/Business Writing: Many companies that have occasional need for skilled writers to prepare the prose for their instruction manuals and sales catalogs don't have staff members who are capable of doing the work. You might build a list of free-lancers who can turn out such writing and then offer their services to all the likely prospects in your area.

Vacant Home Patrol: The tremendous increase in burglaries has homeowners concerned, especially when they must be away from their homes for extended periods. That's why they are eager to enlist the services of vacant home patrols—business firms whose employees make regular stops at the residences to check things out, pick up the mail and newspapers, and generally make the places appear lived-in. You provide this service by hiring retired people who may be seeking an activity that will pay them a few dollars for their efforts.

Waiters/Waitresses: This works very much like the bartenders plan mentioned early in this listing.

Window Washing: Many buildings contain an awful lot of glass which has to be cleaned regularly. The opportunity for profiting from the work of others here should be obvious to you. Enlist the workers, sign up the clients on a contract basis, and you're in business.

HOW TO SELECT, START, AND OPERATE A "PEOPLE" BUSINESS

The six rules you're about to learn will guide you to the proper spare-time money-making business that features the work of other people, starting that business, and then making it quickly profitable. The examples from my files will help to illustrate the points.

FIRST RULE:
Do What You Know or Can Easily Learn

Pick a field you know or can learn easily. Your goal, after all, is to start earning a good spare-time income as quickly as you can. With so many "people" fields to choose from, you should have little difficulty in doing this.

This is not to say that you must have worked in precisely the same type of business before, but you should have a working knowledge of the tasks involved in the service you'll be providing.

> **Example:** Phil T. had played saxophone in a local nightclub group during his younger years, but he had never worked for an entertainment bureau. His knowledge of the entertainment field, however, gave him enough background to start such a bureau.

> **Example:** June C. knew nothing about guided tours, but it was a field she could easily learn by visiting several different cities and going on the various local tours offered. She paid close attention to how the tours were sold and conducted, made detailed notes, and returned home to start a successful tour service in her city.

SECOND RULE:
Favor Business Over Personal Services

You'll note that there are two categories of services contained in our listing: (1) services for business firms, and (2) services for individuals and families. Everything else being equal, your choice should be in the business field, because business services generally pay more, they are easier to sell, and it's often easier to get repeat business from the same clients.

Naturally, you should not rule out personal services. If you spot an outstanding local need, or a field for which you are particularly qualified, then give that first consideration.

Example: Alan N.'s background was in bookkeeping, and he thought of starting either an income tax preparation service for individuals or a bookkeeping service for small companies. He chose the latter because (1) it was not seasonal, (2) less advertising and promotion would be needed, and (3) it was easy to find likely prospects for his service.

Example: Bea W.'s background was also in bookkeeping, but she chose income tax return preparation. In her case it was the wisest choice because (1) she had done a lot of income tax work and had kept up on the latest rules changes, and (2) there was no other personal income tax service in her community.

THIRD RULE:
Sign Up More People Than You Need

Since your idea is to have other people perform the actual service your company is offering, you'll need an ample number of people to do the work. And by "ample" I mean more than you think you'll need. One of the chief factors that convinces people that they should go to work for you is that they have the freedom to accept or not accept assignments. You'll find times—especially during vacation and holiday periods—when a lot of the people on your list are not available for assignment. The bigger your list, the less of a problem this will be.

Example: George B. runs an odd job agency in his town. He signs up young men and women who are willing to do various kinds of physical labor for homeowners and small businesses. At first, the bulk of his work force came from the student body of a local college. But when the first summer vacation time rolled around, George found that most of his odd-jobbers had returned to their homes and were unavailable. Now he includes a lot of high school youngsters as well, and he is never short of help.

FOURTH RULE:
Set Realistic Rates

Many people who start out in a "people" type of service business fail to set rates that are high enough. This is especially true in temporary help fields. You've got to—and the client expects you to—charge more than full-timers in the same field are paid. This is the price the client pays for the convenience of obtaining a qualified person on a temporary basis.

Example: David L., whose story is told earlier in this chapter, charges the going rate for office workers plus one third. That one third is the amount he keeps for himself. Thus, if a typist is paid $3.75 an hour, he charges the client $5.00 an hour for the typist's services. There are two ways to look at it: you charge the worker's hourly rate of pay plus one third, or you pay the worker three fourths of what the client pays you. Either way, it works out to the same amount.

FIFTH RULE:
Avoid Employment Responsibilities

This isn't always possible, but when it is you should do one of the following:

1. Treat the people you sign up as independent contractors. This means that they are working for themselves rather than for you. They are thus responsible for paying their own taxes and you are not responsible for any of the other deductions required of a regular employer.
2. Have the client responsible for whatever employee deductions are required.

Why get involved in more paperwork than you have to? Let the other guy take care of it, and your business will be easier to run and will be more profitable.

Example: The entertainers who get "gigs" through Phil T.'s entertainment bureau are independent contractors. They are not considered legal employees of him or of his clients. They work for themselves, contracting out their entertainment services.

Example: When Cyrus O. sends laborers to companies who need them on a temporary basis, the arrangement is that the laborers are to be considered employees of the client firms. Any income tax, Social Security, and unemployment deductions are made by the employer.

SIXTH RULE:
Utilize Pinpoint Advertising

When you offer a business or personal service, you plan to deal with a relatively small segment of the population. It would be wasteful to advertise your business on a wide scale because you'd be paying to reach a lot of people who have no need for your service.

The goal should be to "pinpoint" your advertising so that it reaches precisely the people who need and are willing to pay for what you have to offer. This means using such advertising methods as classified ads, direct mail, personal visits, phone calls, etc.

Example: Phil T. lets nightclubs and other entertainment clients know of his service by (1) advertising in the Yellow Pages, (2) sending notices to clubs and organizations, and (3) personally contacting the heads of businesses and clubs who make frequent use of hired entertainment.

Example: June C.'s guided tour service is sold primarily through local motels and hotels. Descriptive leaflets are placed in their lobbies. The leaflets contain information on the type and length of each tour, the price, and the times and locations of departure. Hotels and motels are always willing to have local "what-to-do" information displayed in their lobbies. And June has also made special arrangements with several hostelries to have the leaflets placed in each guest room.

MANY OTHER OPPORTUNITIES

You've probably realized this by now: If you want to run an "other-people-do-the-work" type of business, you are not confined to the 50 categories listed in this chapter. The fact is that a great majority of the businesses outlined throughout the book can be run by "remote control."

Develop a workable business plan (maybe doing the actual work by yourself at the start in order to fine-tune the operation) and then turn the labor over to others while you control things from your den or home office. This way the only limit to how big your business can grow is the demand for the product or service that it provides.

6

How to Win with Mail Order

Mail order began as a convenience for residents of rural communities who found it difficult to get into a city to buy items that were not available in the local stores. It has grown to the point where virtually everyone, in the smallest towns and the biggest cities, makes at least occasional purchases by mail.

And not only has just about everybody gotten into the act at the buying end—just about anybody who wants to can get into the act at the selling end. The truth is that a mail order business is among the easiest to start. And if you follow the instructions in this chapter it can become even easier, and the opportunities for success even greater.

LAUNCH A NATIONAL BUSINESS WITH JUST A FEW DOLLARS

One of the great appeals of mail order is its unusual potential for growth. What other business can you think of that has more than 200 million people as potential customers? Examine these other appeals:

- A direct mail business can be started at home as a "kitchen table" operation
- It can be launched with a minimum investment by featuring one product and then quickly expanding to related items
- It's easy to spot successful direct mail businesses and to adopt many of the same high-profit techniques

Gaining these advantages will become much easier when you learn, in this chapter, to do as the direct mail professionals do:

- Pick a proven mail order seller
- Use advertising that brings results
- Gain repeat business from the same customers
- Develop a lifetime source of income

Each of these techniques, and many others employed by highly successful mail order entrepreneurs, can be yours if you follow methods that are surprisingly simple. In fact, you're going to learn how to determine in advance what your own best-selling items will be and how you can best promote them across the country.

HOW $1,100 BUILDS A MAIL ORDER FORTUNE

Perhaps the title of this section should be "How a Pooper Scooper Launches a Mail Order Fortune" because that's the item that started Roger T. on his way to becoming a direct mail millionaire.

"I owned several dogs at the time and I knew what a problem it was keeping our yard clear of dog dirt," Roger recalls. "At first we used a shovel, but that was awkward. Then I saw an ad for a Pooper Scooper in one of the magazines and I sent for it. Shaped something like fireplace tongs, it was just the thing I needed. I'm surprised I had never seen one before. I checked the stores and, sure enough, some of them carried these items. But I figured that if I had never come across them on the display racks, many other pet lovers hadn't either."

Spotting an opportunity, Roger wrote to the manufacturer whose label was on the item he had bought from the pet supply house and obtained a price list for wholesale quantities. He also obtained prices from a number of manufacturers of other pet-line items.

"I decided to feature the Pooper Scooper in some initial test advertising. Using a line drawing contained in the manufacturer's catalog to illustrate the item, I inserted a small ad in one of the back pages of a women's magazine. The ad brought enough sales to pay for the wholesale cost of the product and for the advertising itself. But there wasn't any real profit—just enough to break even. I figured I must be doing something wrong."

Roger soon found that he wasn't doing anything wrong at all. He realized this when the retail mail order firm from whom he had bought his first Pooper Scooper sent him a catalog of pet items.

"It suddenly dawned on me," Roger remembers, "that the money was probably made in second and third sales to customers obtained through the original ad. What that retailer was doing, I reasoned, was advertising a useful item in the magazines and then following it up by sending catalogs out to people who bought it."

What Roger discovered was that mail order professionals rarely expect to make money with the first sale. They use that sale to build a customer list, for it is a proven fact that once you have satisfied customers you can sell similar items to them time and time again. The initial item is something like the "loss leader" that supermarkets and department stores advertise in order to get customers into the stores. These merchants realize that once a person is in the store he or she will probably buy a number of other items as well.

Roger's initial stock of merchandise cost him $300. The tiny ad cost $450. When he realized that he needed a catalog or "flyer" with which to promote other pet items, he spent $300 to have one printed. Another $50 went for incidental expenses such as postage, wrapping materials, etc. Thus, for $1,100 he had the start of what soon became a going concern.

"Since I got my advertising and product money back from the first batch of sales, I immediately reinvested that cash in more stock and more advertising. Rather than go the cost of mailing out a catalog separately, I included the flyer with each product mailed out to a customer. This generated additional sales—and continued doing so until I had enough money to get a small but impressive catalog printed. I then mailed this to all of the people who had bought from me."

Roger now mails his catalogs several times a year, and his customer list numbers several hundred thousand. The business is conservatively worth more than a million dollars. The story of his success would not be surprising to any of today's other mail order entrepreneurs. It's been done many times, in many different fields, with the same basic methods. The key is to pick the right type of product and know how and where to advertise it—knowledge that you will gain as you progress through this chapter.

50 PROVEN MAIL ORDER SPECIALTIES

Many thousands of items can be (and are being) successfully sold through the mail. A list of 50 specialties is far from complete, but all of the items included in this list are proven money-makers in the direct mail business. Pick one of these as a starter and you'll know that you have a solid foundation on which to build your business.

As in earlier chapters, some of the listings are followed by brief comments. Other listings, which should be self-explanatory, stand alone.

Apparel: Items of clothing have long been top mail order sellers, especially when the customer is offered unusual items that are not readily available in local stores.

Art Reproductions: One key to success in selling any mail order item is the ability to show the customer exactly what he is getting. Art being art, the customer has no doubt about what he's getting when the work is adequately illustrated in your ad or catalog.

Artists' Supplies: Hobbyists comprise one of the biggest categories of mail order buyers. Artists and craftsmen are also excellent people to cater to because they are repeat buyers. Their supplies run out, and if they liked what they got from you the first time, they'll buy again and again.

Athletic Equipment: Read the explanation under "Artists' Supplies" and you'll know why athletic equipment is also a top mail order seller.

Auto Supplies: With the high cost of auto repairs—and a growing "do-it-yourself" segment in our society—mail order houses dealing in parts and gadgets for cars and vans are doing exceedingly well.

Books: Books which cater to people with special interests are the key here. An added advantage to the dealer is that the post office allows you to mail them with much less postage than that required for most other types of parcels.

Burglar Alarms

Calculators: To be successful in this field, you've got to offer an item with special features. It's hard to compete with the $8 and $10 bargains in the stores if you're offering the same thing. But pick one of the growing number of calculators that do out-of-the-ordinary jobs and you may have yourself a winner.

Cameras

Camping Supplies: See the explanation under "Artists' Supplies." The same thing applies here.

Candy

Coats of Arms: The popularity of the book and TV miniseries, *Roots*, has brought about a renewed interest in family lines.

Hence the popularity of colorful coats of arms displayed by families who wish to boast about their real (or imagined) family heritage.

Coins

Construction Plans: Once you compile (or buy the rights to) construction plans they can be reproduced inexpensively and sold at a tremendous markup. Mail order businesses are selling construction plans for everything from homes to log cabins, airplanes, helicopters, boats, dollhouses, grandfather clocks, and just about any other buildable item you can think of.

Cookware

Custom Photo Finishing: You can't compete with the "cheapie" developing houses that develop rolls of film by running them through a computerized machine, but you can make money by catering to serious photographers who want custom work. You charge more, and they're willing to pay it.

Do-It-Yourself Kits: I went into considerable detail about this in an earlier chapter. Do-it-yourself kits are successful for the same reasons that construction plans, as listed above, are successful.

Employment Information: Some companies have been in business for years selling information about overseas employment or jobs in specialized fields. Be very careful, however, that you do not mislead your customers. The government keeps a vigilant eye on employment opportunity ads.

Energy Conservation Items: Everyone knows the importance of conserving our energy resources, and some people actually do something about it. A number of manufacturers are putting out products geared at this market. Latch on to several of these items as listings in a small catalog and you may have the basis of a successful mail order business.

Fishing Tackle

Games & Toys

Garden Supplies

Gifts: This is probably the most popular category of small catalog sales. It's also a highly competitive field, so you've got to pick and choose carefully.

Gourmet Food Items: Many gourmet foods are mailable, and many people do buy gourmet foods by mail. This is a great repeat order business.

Health Foods

Hobby Supplies

Instruction: This can be in the form of books, cassette tapes, diagrams, and now, with modern technology, tapes for home TV recorders and personal computers. The human quest for knowledge never ends, and regular schools and adult education programs can't begin to fill the gap for the unusual types of learning many people seek.

Jewelry

Magic Tricks: It's safe to say that the majority of manufactured magic tricks are sold through the mail, and not just to kids, either. There's a sizable segment of the adult population who are interested in this hobby.

Mailing Lists: This is more a mail order sideline than a mail order business, but it's a highly profitable sideline. Once you have built up a list of customers with several thousand names (five or ten thousand is the preferred minimum) you can then rent that list to other mail order firms. It's all handled very neatly for you through list brokers, who charge a commission for their services. Such brokers advertise regularly in a magazine called *Direct Marketing,* whose address is 224 Seventh St., Garden City, N.Y. 11530.

Manuscript Typing: Many free-lance writers are not nearly as good at typing as they are at composing the words to be typed. That's why they turn to professional typists—many of whom advertise in the writers' magazines.

Musical Instruments

Nautical Accessories

Newsletters: Chapter 9 goes into this big-potential field in detail.

Novelties

Office Supplies: Many companies buy nearly all their office supplies (paper, ribbons, carbons, printed forms, etc.) through the mail. Many other companies are in the direct mail office supply business, but there's room for more.

Personal Computer Programs: The growing interest in home computers has led to a giant need for software—programs that can be entered into these computers to make them more useful to the owners. If you have a hobby computer and know how to program games, checkbook balancers, etc., you can sell your programs to fellow enthusiasts. There are half a dozen home computer magazines in which these programs can be advertised.

Personalized Items: Just about everyone loves his or her own name (or at least likes to see it prominently displayed) and that's why personalized items are so popular. Most stores can't be bothered with handling such business, so the bulk of the work goes to mail order firms. Your imagination is the only limit on what can be offered and sold through the mail to buyers of personalized items.

Pet Supplies

Plants

Printing: Just as with office supplies, many companies and individuals get most of their printing done through the mail. Thanks to quick and inexpensive delivery by United Parcel Service, it's a practical and economical alternative to having printing jobs done locally.

Purebred Dogs: Yes, these are indeed mail order items. Many breeders ship all over the country. It takes special preparation and handling, of course, but for dogs from champion stock, the income makes it all worthwhile.

Records & Tapes

Religious Items

Rubber Stamps

Shoes

Stamps for Collectors

Telephone Answering Machines: This used to be a better mail order seller than it is now, because the devices have become available in many stores. But if you find a manufacturer who has one with unique features that are not usually available "around the corner" you can still cash in on the growing market.

Tools

Watches: This, after all, is how Richard Sears started out. Many years later, the item that got the Sears Roebuck firm on its feet is still an excellent seller by mail.

HOW TO PICK THE RIGHT MAIL ORDER PRODUCT OR SERVICE

There are two powerful rules for picking a mail order product or service. By consistently sticking to these guidelines, mail order professionals find one winner after another. Not knowing these rules, or not realizing how effective they are, beginners often ignore them and wonder why they are not successful.

Perhaps the reason that beginners ignore the rules is that they seem so simple that mail order newcomers doubt their effectiveness. Believe me, they work, and I'm going to demonstrate it to you. Here are the two rules:

1. *Pick a product or service field that deeply interests you.*
2. *Narrow down your selection to items that are closely similar to items already being sold through the mail.*

Simple? Yes. Easy? Fairly so. But you'd be surprised at how many people ignore these time-proven product-picking techniques and try to be the first to sell something entirely new through the mail. You'll see shortly why that's not the wise thing to do. Let's look a bit closer at each of the rules.

The First Product Selection Rule

There are several reasons why it's important to pick a product or service that deeply interests you. Here are some of them:

1. People tend to know a lot more about things that interest them than about things they don't particularly care for. The more you know about your field, the better businessperson you'll be.
2. When you like your product, your enthusiasm has to be evident in the advertising you prepare, and this will help you to sell your product or service.
3. If the field really fascinates you, you'll find it no annoyance to keep up to date on the latest developments—and this keeps you on top in the marketplace.

Todd M. learned the first product selection rule the hard way. While attending a regional trade show, he spotted a unique gardening tool that he thought he could sell through the mail. He bought up a supply, inserted some ads in gardening magazines, and then waited for the orders to pour in.

"Well, the orders did come in," Todd says, "but so did the product returns. People who bought the item didn't like it. I was giving refunds on more than half the items sold." Todd soon found that you can't make money that way.

Thinking about it, he soon found that he was in the wrong field.

Mail order wasn't wrong—but the product line he had chosen was.

"I had never gardened in my life," he recalls. "If I had, I probably would have known that this 'gimmicky' garden aid was not practical. Real gardeners soon found that it didn't live up to its promise."

Todd vowed then and there to stick to what he knew and liked. Then he'd be able to test a product himself and know before he offered it for sale whether other people who shared his interests would be willing to pay for it—and keep it, rather than demanding a refund.

What did he know and like?

"Well, my family and I love to take vacations in our motor home," he reports. "And I'm constantly poring through the recreational vehicle magazines looking for new doodads to add to our vehicle. Of course, thousands of other people are doing the same thing. So that's the mail order field I decided to try next."

His first item was a magazine rack that attaches to the wall—something you don't often see in private homes but which is very handy in the more cramped space of motor homes. It sold well, and Todd soon added other items to his motor home product line. He now issues a catalog to his growing customer list about three times a year—spring, mid-summer, and just before the holiday season. He's learned from personal experience that the first product selection rule can help you pick the mail order items that will work best for you.

The Second Product Selection Rule

Pick items similar to what is already being successfully sold through the mail and half of your work will have already been done for you. Millions of dollars are spent each year on testing mail order products to determine what will sell and what won't. For every product that sells profitably, there are probably at least half a dozen that don't make money.

So why go through all the bother of testing the half dozen non-saleable items until you find one that hits? In other words, why not let other people do your homework for you?

You get other people to do your homework by closely watching the ads. Pay particular heed to the ads that are repeated month after month. This means that the item or service being offered is making money—or else the advertiser would not be able to continue the ad.

This applies not only to publication advertising but also to direct mail ads. You can get yourself on numerous mailing lists in your chosen field merely by responding to a number of "coupon" ads and subscribing to special interest magazines that cover the field. The "inquiry" lists and subscription lists will soon be offered by the advertisers for rental to other firms, and you'll be receiving all kinds of mail from various firms selling items in that field.

When you see products or services offered over and over again by the same firm and by competing firms over a period of many months, then you know that those companies have to be making money at it.

Mail order, as they say, is an open book. Because of the very nature of the business, no one can hide his success. If a product is successful, all of the interested mail order competitors soon know it, and some of the smart ones jump on the bandwagon. And that's all the more reason why you should not go to the considerable trouble and expense of discovering and then introducing an entirely new product line. Once you achieve success, others will spot it and will move in, capitalizing on all of your hard work.

Since in most mail order fields there's room for everybody, why don't you be the smart one—and let other people do the research?

Many years ago, one of America's most successful mail order entrepreneurs told me:

> *"For every mail order success that stems from innovation,
> there are a hundred that result from imitation."*

So why not put the odds in your favor? Choose a product or service that is already being successfully sold through the mail and your chances of success will be much greater.

A STEP-BY-STEP GUIDE TO STARTING AND RUNNING YOUR DIRECT MAIL BUSINESS

Once you've decided on a product line (remember that one product is not enough—the real profits come from follow-up sales to the same customers) here are the steps that will set you up in your mail order business:

1. Prepare your advertising.
2. Set up a record-keeping system.
3. Use professional testing techniques.

4. Always have something more to sell.

5. Earn extra income through list rentals.

We'll deal with these steps, one by one.

STEP ONE:
Prepare Your Advertising

The first thing most mail order newcomers want to know after they've settled on what they're going to sell is how and where they should advertise. Established professionals don't have to ask this question because they already know the answer. Just as in picking a product, there is a simple, direct, highly effective solution.

How and where should you advertise your product or service? Here's the rule you should follow now and for as long as you are in the mail order business:

Make your advertising closely similar to that of your competitors.

Some people call it the "copycat technique" and it works for the same reason that the second product selection rule works. You've chosen your product on the basis of what is already being successfully sold through the mail, and it stands to reason that what works with product selection works equally well with product advertising. When other firms selling similar products or services consistently run a certain type of ad, you know that it has to be pulling in orders for them.

Thus:

- If they sell by sending out mailed circulars . . .
- If they sell with coupon advertising in magazines . . .
- If they use publication advertising merely to obtain inquiries, closing the deal with follow-up letters . . .

. . . then that is precisely the method that you should use. You can bet your last postage stamp that many of these same advertisers have tried different methods. What they've settled on as being the most successful is the method you see employed month in, month out. In other words, the ads keep running because they work.

Naturally, ethics require that you not copy advertising word for word, layout for layout. In fact, many ads are copyrighted. But you can create the same type of advertising appeal with different words; and if you can't do it, then hire one of the mail order copywriters who advertise in *Direct Mail Magazine*.

STEP TWO:
Set Up a Record-Keeping System

The most valuable assets in any mail order operation are its records—especially the records which contain the names and addresses of customers. Your customer list is your key to continued profits. If you lose it, it's almost like having to start all over again from scratch.

The customer list is so valuable that many mail order firms keep a duplicate copy in a separate location, such as a safe deposit box.

Nearly as valuable, but on a shorter term basis, are the records you keep of:

- Orders received from individual ads
- Orders received from individual mailing campaigns
- Orders received from catalogs included with product shipments
- Sales volumes for each product you offer
- Receipts and expenses for tax purposes

Armed with the information contained in these records and guided by the special testing techniques you are about to learn, you can build a steadily growing business that will provide you with the big income you seek.

It really doesn't matter what kind of charts or forms you set up for the purpose of keeping these records, as long as they are clear and provide you with quick access to the information you need. One thing is vital, though, and that is "keying" your advertisements in such a way that whenever an order is received, you'll know what ad or direct mail piece prompted the order.

You've probably noticed the special codes on many order coupons. They let the advertiser know exactly which ad the buyer is responding to. In cases where the advertisement does not contain a coupon or order form, a special code number is usually included in the address. Examine the following:

American Gift Corporation
Dept. 11L
100 Main Street
Anytown, USA 00000

The second line is the key. This particular code might, for example, tell American Gift Corporation that the ad appeared in the November issue of *Ladies Home Journal*. Other companies key their ads by adding a letter to their street number.

Now that you know how to key an ad or sales letter, let's see how you can use the information it provides to give your advertising its best possible pulling power.

STEP THREE:
Use Professional Testing Techniques

If records are your most valuable assets in a mail order operation, then testing is your most powerful technique. Without testing, few mail order companies could last very long.

Why? Because no one, not even the most seasoned mail order veteran, knows in advance how well a product or an advertisement will sell. But he knows how to estimate with a great deal of accuracy. He does this by testing.

I can sense that you have a question. "Why should I have to test," you inquire, "when you say that by imitating ads of other companies I'm already on the right track?"

You are on the right track . . . but you want to stay on the track, don't you? The advertising run by other companies should be your guide, but you've got to develop your advertising so that it works best for *you*. And you can only do that by running small test ads and seeing how they pull.

Here are some examples of how big companies test their advertising:

- A company that sells leather goods places its test ad in a regional edition of a national magazine. If it generates enough sales, the ad is then run in the national edition of the same publication.

- A phonograph record club that is considering sending out mailing pieces to a list of 1.5 million names tests the list by sending its literature to a five or ten percent sampling of the names on that list.

- The publisher of a home study course isn't sure whether to charge $39.50 or $49.50 for the course. So he conducts an "A–B" test in which the mailing list is divided into halves, the "A" section and the "B" section. The product is offered to people on the "A" half of the list for $39.50, and to people on the "B" half of the list for $49.50. Then the publisher determines which price is more profitable to use.

Believe it or not, mail order advertisers do occasionally find it more profitable to charge a higher price. In some cases the drop in sales volume is more than offset by the increase in dollar volume. That is one of the many values of testing.

How Testing Pays Off

"If it weren't for testing, I wouldn't be a wealthy man today." That statement comes from Ken D., who launched a direct mail business specializing in camping supplies about five years ago. "My advertising tests have told me in advance what mailing lists I should use, what products I should offer as a means of gaining new customers, how big my magazine ads should be, and how often they should run."

Starting with just a couple of items advertised in a small magazine, Ken has built a business that issues several catalogs a year, with sales reaching into millions of dollars.

"As an example of how testing has helped me," Ken says, "I found that in a certain well-known national magazine I get more for my advertising dollar by running a quarter-page ad every other month than by running the same ad monthly. My tests showed that when the ad ran for two consecutive months, it pulled a lot of orders the first month but this was followed by a sharp drop the next month, and an even bigger drop the third month.

"Then, when I switched to an every-other-month basis, the sales volume hit a steady, satisfactory level."

In other cases, tests have shown Ken that smaller ads sometimes pull just as well as bigger ads. "You can imagine how much money that knowledge has saved me," he states.

As a beginner, you naturally cannot afford to conduct extensive testing campaigns. That's why I say that your initial advertising should be similar in style to what existing firms are doing. Thus you are capitalizing on their own testing. But even from the start you can test on a small scale.

You can, for example, insert different ads rather than the same one when you decide to advertise in the same magazine for several months. Make a note of which ad pulls best.

If your advertising is to be done through the mail, you can order a test from the mailing list broker rather than an entire list. Everyone who rents mailing lists allows you to use a small part of the list for testing purposes before deciding whether or not to go ahead with the entire list.

The relatively low cost of printing sales letters allows you to write two or more letters advertising the same product or service. Split up the names on the list to which the letters are to be sent, sending one letter to the "A" names and the other to the "B" names. You may be surprised at the results. One letter, perhaps even the one you thought was the weaker of the two, might far outpull the other.

STEP FOUR:
Always Have Something More to Sell

Since your prime asset in a direct mail business is your list of customers, you should capitalize on that asset to the fullest. It's a demonstrated fact that any mail order operator can make two, three, or even four times as many sales to his customer list than he can to a "cold" list of names rented from some other source. That's because customers

- Are familiar with the firm and pay more attention to the mail it sends them
- Have shown that they are already interested in the product or service because they have purchased it in the past
- Trust the firm because (1) it has sent them something they are pleased with or (2) it has cheerfully honored their request for a refund

Once you have assembled enough customer names to warrant sending out a mailing to them, what is it that you should offer? That depends on the nature of your original product or service. Follow these guidelines:

1. If yours is a "replenishable" product (something that the customer will need refilled or replaced in the future), you should send him periodic reminders that you are ready to continue serving him.
2. If the initial product sold to a customer is a "one-time" item (one that does not need replacement or replenishing), then similar or related items should be offered next.
3. Services are sold on a similar basis. If the customer is satisfied with your past service (and you should make every

effort to make him so) then he should be reminded periodically that you stand ready to serve him again. If it's a "one-time" type of service, then have other similar services to offer from time to time.

We'll look briefly at how successful mail order business owners are gaining repeat business in each of these three categories.

- *Replenishable Products.* Susan Z. sells artists' supplies. She solicits her customers through "one-item" ads in magazines, offering a bargain in paints or brushes or easels. Then, several times each year her customers are sent a small catalog listing all of the art items she has for sale. "More than 65% of my customers are repeat buyers," Susan reports.

- *One-Time Products.* Randy B. specializes in personalized products. His magazine advertising, aimed at building up his customer list, offers an attractive door plaque imprinted with the customer's name. "Since most people need only one door plaque for their home or apartment, I make new sales to the same people by sending them literature on such personalized items as lawn signs, desk nameplates, holiday cards, stationery, memo pads, and even monogrammed handkerchiefs," Randy notes. "To increase business even more, I suggest that my customers consider some of these items as gifts for their friends and relatives."

- *Service.* Steve C. does mail order printing, specializing in business forms such as invoices, billheads, and packing lists. "Naturally, my customers need these items repeatedly. And since I offer competitive prices and fast service, they get their refills from me. But to prod them on I send out price lists about twice a year," he states.

These people are successful because they follow the tried-and-true mail order formula: They gain new customers by offering one attractively priced mail order product or service, and they keep customers by making sure that they always have something else to sell the same customers.

STEP FIVE:
Earn Extra Income Through List Rentals

Your customer list is your prime asset in more ways than one. It is, of course, the mainstay of your own mail order operation. But it can also be a means of added profit when you offer it for rental to other firms. And you do this by arranging with a list broker to include it in the broker's catalog of available lists.

"But can't it hurt my business if my list is offered to competitors?" That's a question I'm frequently asked. It is true that you probably won't want to allow firms that are in direct competition to use your lists, as they could steal away some of your customers. But when you offer a list for rental, you have the final say on who can use it and who can't. You can also stipulate that you must have prior approval over the advertising pieces that are sent to people on your list.

"What about stealing my names?" That's another frequently asked question. If it bothers you, you can arrange it so that the renters never see the names. You can handle the addressing and mailing for them—at an additional charge, of course. Or, you can insert "code names" on your list—names of friends or relatives. If the friends or relatives receive more letters from the list renter than the renter has paid for, you know right away that he's cheating.

How profitable can list rentals be? Well, at an average fee of $35 per thousand names it can be quite profitable, with very little work involved. Let's say that you have 50,000 names on your list and that the list is rented 20 times a year. That's $35,000 in bonus income.

7

Cash In On the Seminar and Training Boom

There are more money-making opportunities in the seminar and training fields than in almost any other category described in this book. These are such broad-based fields that, regardless of your background and experience, there's a highly profitable slot that you can fill.

First, let's define the two terms as we'll use them in this chapter:

Seminars are one, two, or three-day sessions in which groups of people gain specialized knowledge to help them in their work.

Training involves a series of classes spread over several weeks or months, and in some cases even longer, that are conducted either on an individual basis or in a classroom. The subject matter can be almost anything from employment and business skills to hobby and sports interests.

Why do I say that there are so many opportunities in these two related fields? Because you can conduct a seminar or a training course on almost any subject; there are literally thousands to choose from. Experience you've gained in your job or hobby pursuits can be "sold" to others—at a handsome profit.

Even if you don't happen to have specialized knowledge or experience that you feel is worth selling, you can still cash in on the seminar and training boom by hiring people who do have such knowledge. They get paid at an hourly rate and you get to keep the big profits involved.

AMERICANS SHELL OUT BIG MONEY FOR KNOWLEDGE

The American quest for knowledge has never been greater. No one has ever been able to estimate how many billions of dollars are spent each year on obtaining the knowledge we all seem to crave, because we buy it in so many different forms—books, magazines, schools, home study courses, tutoring, newsletters, radio and TV, etc. One thing is known: It comprises a significant portion of nearly everybody's budget.

I have good news for you. You can take part in the boom with an investment of under $1,500. By using rented space (or the customer's own home or office) and meeting some incidental operating expenses, you can build a business that makes more money than most "small" businesspeople ever dream of. Most people don't realize how easy and inexpensive it is to launch a seminar or training project, but after reading this chapter you won't be "most people" and you'll be able to latch onto one of today's most beckoning opportunities.

HOW $650 PAYS FOR A $2,000-PER-WEEK BUSINESS

Frank G. was a car salesman and a good one—but not quite good enough to keep his boss from going bankrupt. In fact, there's probably not a salesman in the world good enough to have prevented that. Bad policy decisions had made bankruptcy unavoidable, and they also put Frank out of a job.

"I wasn't worried about being unemployed," Frank recalls. "My reputation as a highly successful salesman was well known and I had several job offers. But something one of the dealers said to me made me decide against taking another job.

"He said to me, 'Frank, I want you to be my sales manager. You know more about selling than anybody I have working for me, and you could teach my men a lot.' It was that last part that started me thinking. If I could teach his men a lot, then I could teach a lot of men a lot."

And that's what Frank set out to do. He recalled a sales seminar his former boss had sent him to several years previously. It was held in the banquet room of a motel located in a nearby city.

"If I remember right, he paid $300 for my participation in the three-day seminar. There were about 50 of us attending from car agencies located throughout the area. Simple multiplication showed me that they took in $15,000 for that three-day event. Why couldn't I conduct sales training seminars and rake in that kind of money?"

He could and he did. He decided not to confine his subject matter to selling cars, but to sales in general.

"Selling is selling, I maintain. It takes the same skill to sell a refrigerator as it does to sell a car or a piece of real estate. Naturally, the salesperson has to have a basic knowledge of the item he's dealing with—but after that good salesmanship is good salesmanship."

SELLING A SALES SEMINAR

Frank invested $650 in some stationery and a brochure, a business telephone, and an answering machine. Then, making use of his own sales ability, he hit the road and visited with managers of companies that employed large numbers of salesmen.

"I told them about a seminar I was planning to hold at a centrally located Holiday Inn. It would be three days long and the fee would be $300. I told them of the techniques I had developed during my own sales career and how I could impart some of those success techniques to their own key salespeople."

Within a week, Frank had 50 enrollees in his course. The deposit he received more than paid for the meeting room and the luncheons that were included in the seminar, along with some books he handed out as part of the course. His net profit for the event was more than $11,000.

"I now conduct similar seminars throughout my section of the country," Frank reports. "They average about one every five or six weeks. What do I do the rest of the time? Well, part of that time is spent in administrative work and signing up participating companies. The rest of it is spent on the golf course. I'm essentially a part-timer—and I'm clearing better than $100,000 a year. It sure beats selling cars."

YOU DON'T HAVE TO BE A PROMOTER OR EVEN AN EXPERT

I'll concede that being a top-notch salesman made it easy for Frank in two ways. He has valuable knowledge that other people are willing to pay well for. And, being a salesman, it's been easy for him to convince companies to sign up their personnel for his seminars.

But the truth is that you don't have to be either an expert or a promoter to be successful in the seminar business. Here are two very interesting factors about the seminar industry:

- Many seminars are not taught by the people who sponsor them. Instead, the sponsors hire experts in the field. There's more than enough profit to pay for this.
- Most seminars are not "sold" in person at all. Enrollees are signed up entirely through the mail.

The experience of Maria V. demonstrates the point. Realizing that more and more well-to-do people were seeking to invest some of their money in art as a hedge against inflation, Maria knew they could benefit from impartial advice on how to go about investing in art.

"Too many of them had been stung by promoters who wanted to sell them a specific type of collectible," Maria asserts. "What they needed was good, solid advice from experts who had nothing to sell them but knowledge."

Was Maria one of those experts? "Certainly not. I knew very little about art. But I realized that by paying well, I could sign up people who were experts to give lectures at seminars I sponsored."

Nor is Maria a salesperson or promoter able to go out and convince people to sign up for her course. "I get tongue-tied when I try to sell something," Maria admits. "So I did what most other seminar sponsors do—I rented some mailing lists and sent out literature to likely prospects."

Maria's seminars are conducted in many of the country's larger cities. She picks art investment experts from each city to give lectures at the one-day affairs, paying each lecturer an average of $100.

"For a panel of five experts, it costs me about $500. I charge $200 for the seminar, and average about 50 enrollees. Subtract rent, teaching fees, sales costs, and administrative expenses from the $10,000 I take in, and the profit per session still amounts to more than $6,000."

THE DIFFERENCES BETWEEN SEMINARS AND TRAINING

The basic difference between seminars and training involves time and location. As you've already read, seminars are usually one-, two-, or three-day affairs, and training can extend over a period of months or, in some cases, even years. Also, the seminar business is a traveling business, while training is usually performed at a fixed location.

Generally, the same seminar can be given in the same city only

once or twice a year; thus the sponsors move their operations from city
to city, arranging next month's sessions while this month's are being
conducted. But a training course can be given continuously in the same
location. That's because it is designed to appeal to a greater number of
people, and you don't run out of "customers" after one or two courses
have been given.

But in a way, training is similar to seminar-conducting. If you are
successful in conducting a course in one city, you can probably open up
branches in many other cities as well. Well known examples of branch-
oriented "training" businesses are the Berlitz School of Languages,
Weight Watchers, Smokenders, and the Dale Carnegie Course. You'll
find them throughout the country.

BRANCH OUT FOR SUCCESS

Several years ago, Ted G. installed dual controls in his automobile
and started a driving school in his home town. It quickly caught on, and
he added more vehicles and some part-time instructors.

"But there came a point where I was saturating the market," Ted
reports. "There was only enough business in that particular area to
support three cars and three instructors. Being an ambitious person, I
looked for new areas to conquer. And I found them in several other
communities in the region. I now operate a total of five driving schools,
maintaining a fleet of 20 cars."

In each of the branch locations, one of the instructors serves as the
manager, receiving a percentage of that branch's total receipts in addition to his or her salary as an instructor. This provides an incentive to
drum up business, and it leaves Ted with only a minimum of administrative details to deal with.

Thus the decision on whether you'll be launching a business based
on seminars or on training will depend on:

- The type of knowledge you are selling
- The number of potential students in one location
- Your willingness to travel from city to city

We'll deal with each of the categories separately, outlining some of
the opportunities available to you and explaining how you can get your
business under way.

25 HIGHLY PROFITABLE SEMINAR FIELDS

There are literally thousands of subjects that can be profitably
taught in seminar form. In fact, many of the individual subjects I am
about to list for you are really categories that cover a broad range of

related subjects. The listing will, however, provide you with an insight into what is being done—and what you might be able to do—in the seminar field.

You'll find that most of the seminar topics are geared for business and professional people, because they are the people who need to keep current on the latest developments affecting their businesses, and also because they are willing to pay the relatively steep fees charged by those who conduct seminars.

Accounting: Seminars are not used to train people to become accountants; rather they are highly successful in (1) bringing accountants up-to-date on the latest laws, regulations, and procedures, and (2) helping businesspeople to gain a better understanding of what their accounting departments do or should be doing.

Advertising: This comprises one of the top seminar fields because advertising is so vital to the success of most businesses. There are seminars for people who work in advertising and for businessmen who need a greater insight into what advertising can do for them.

Art Investments

Banking: Bankers are continually attending seminars, many of them sponsored by non-profit banking associations; but because of the growing complexity of today's banking world, the non-profit groups can't keep up with everything, and thus commercial seminars are catching on.

Business Management: Name practically any business field and you have the prospect for a profitable seminar.

Data Processing: There are new developments in this field almost every day. Seminars are used to keep those working in data processing informed about what's happening.

Exporting and Importing: Every business owner is looking for new markets and many want to locate new sources of products they can sell; hence the popularity of seminars conducted by people who know the ropes of exporting and importing.

Fund-Raising: While most non-profit "do-good" organizations know how to perform their functions very well, many are not particularly good at raising funds to pay for their work. That's why they send their key people to fund-raising seminars.

Government Contracts: With the government becoming a bigger part of our lives, it's spending a lot more money in the private sector. Naturally, the smart businessman wants to learn how to tap some of these funds. Seminars on this subject are well attended.

Labor Relations: Due to the increasing power of organized labor, operators of small and medium-sized businesses need more know-how on negotiating contracts and dealing with labor disputes. One way to get this information is to attend a seminar or two.

Mail Order: There are scores of individual topics on which mail order seminars are based. Some deal with copywriting, others with such things as mailing lists, printing, and product selection.

Marketing: To increase profits, many businesses look to new methods of selling their products and services. Retailers look to direct mail; direct mail people investigate placing items in the stores, and so forth. To learn how to do these things, they attend marketing seminars.

Municipal Management: Governmental officials need to keep up-to-date just as much as leaders in the private sector do.

Personnel Management

Planning and Zoning: Community planning often involves creative thinking. To spark their creative juices—and to learn what other communities have done successfully—municipal planners are great seminar attendees.

Public Relations: Business is bad-mouthed so much in the news media these days that forward-looking businessmen must learn how to deal with the press and build up their corporate images.

Publishing: This is another business field that has generated a number of different seminars, including newsletter-publishing, maintaining subscription lists, and attracting advertisers.

Real Estate: Always an attractive type of investment, real estate is a subject many people want to learn more about. Usually seminars deal with one particular phase of real estate, such as investing in or managing apartment houses, subdividing land, or obtaining government backing.

Sales

Security: Shoplifting is such a major problem in today's marketplace that many business owners seek to learn new ways to deal with it. Internal security—preventing thefts by employees—is also a successful seminar subject.

Stock Investments: It is true that a number of stock brokerage firms conduct free seminars on this subject, but many investors consider these seminars "suspect" because they know the broker is trying to sell them something. That's why a growing number of investors attend independent seminars, confident that all the sponsor is selling them is knowledge.

Tax Planning

Travel Promotion

Urban Affairs

Wealth-Building: This is one type of seminar that is aimed not so much at the businessperson as it is at the non-businessperson who would like to become successful in business. These sessions are generally inspirational in nature, featuring lecturers who know how to motivate people into carrying out their long-held money-making dreams.

A STEP-BY-STEP GUIDE TO STARTING A SEMINAR BUSINESS

Because seminars are such brief affairs, they can be planned and conducted in your spare time. There are six steps involved:

1. Choose your field.
2. Lay out the course.
3. Reserve a meeting room.
4. Prepare your advertising.
5. Conduct a prototype session.
6. Guide your expansion.

Let's examine these steps individually to see how they can lead you to cash in on the full profit potential of today's seminar boom.

STEP ONE:
Pick Your Field

Actually, there are two decisions to make here. The first, of course, involves the subject matter on which your seminars will be based. The second deals with who will do the lecturing—you or people you hire.

Whether you conduct the seminars personally or not, they should be based on a field in which you have at least some knowledge. If you don't do the lecturing or teaching yourself, you need not be an expert. But you should be somewhat familiar with the field. You need this familiarity to guide you in laying out the sessions and planning your advertising.

Leonard Z. was far from an expert on tax planning when he chose that as his seminar subject. But he knew that the subject was of vital importance to many people and would be easy to "sell" in seminar form. To gain a slightly better working knowledge of the field, he read some books and subscribed to some newsletters on the subject. Then he contacted a number of tax experts in his area to serve as instructors at his initial session.

The session went well, and it led to what is now a series of seminars conducted in a number of major cities. Leonard has three full-time instructors on his staff who travel from city to city. He goes along with them to handle administrative details.

STEP TWO:
Lay Out the Course

The best way to learn how to conduct a seminar is to attend a seminar—preferably several. Admittedly, this can be expensive when they sell for $200-$300 each. But it's part of your investment and well worthwhile.

You can learn about forthcoming seminars by subscribing to trade magazines in the field you are dealing with. Leonard Z. got himself on the subscription list of several tax accountant and general business publications.

"I not only scoured the trade mags for seminar ads, I soon was receiving mailing pieces from seminar sponsors who rented the magazines' subscription lists," Leonard reports.

What if you can't find any nearby seminars on your particular topic? Attend any seminar you can find. The methods of operation are similar in most fields despite the differing subject matter. Regardless of what business or professional seminar you attend, you'll pick up solid ideas on conducting your own sessions.

STEP THREE:
Reserve a Meeting Room

"Believe it or not, this was the hardest part," Leonard reports. "It meant I was committing myself to going ahead with the project when I was still very nervous about it. But I did it, and of course it marked a major change in my life. I called the manager of a large motel in town and reserved his meeting room for a date several months in advance."

As happened in Leonard's case, you'll probably have to put down a deposit to hold the room. Fifty dollars or so should cover it, with the balance to be paid at the time of your seminar.

STEP FOUR:
Prepare Your Advertising

Again, you'll learn from other seminar sponsors. The ads they run in trade publications and the direct mail pieces they send out will be your guide. Incidentally, the mailing "package" usually consists of a form letter, a brochure outlining the course contents, and a reservation card for the enrollees to mail back to you along with their deposit (or the entire fee, although requiring only a deposit in advance will help you sell more "seats").

"Knowing that if my first seminar was successful I'd be sponsoring many more," Leonard notes, "I had the printer design the brochure so that new dates and locations could be inserted on subsequent reprints. So each time a new seminar is planned, only that information has to be changed. This cuts way down on the cost of printing."

How do you get names and addresses of local people who might be interested in your seminar? From sources such as these:

- Trade magazine subscription lists
- "Compiled" lists containing names of people who work in the field
- Telephone listings
- Association membership lists
- Responses to ads that you run in trade publications

The magazine subscription lists and the compiled lists can be rented through a mailing list broker. *Direct Marketing Magazine* carries names and addresses of such brokers.

STEP FIVE:
Conduct a Prototype Session

"I was pretty confident when the time came to hold my first seminar," Leonard reports. "I had done my homework, hired some good people to conduct the session, and had 45 enrollees signed up."

Nevertheless, there were a few minor, unexpected hitches. That's why you should schedule just one session to begin with. It gives you an opportunity to work out the hitches before scheduling other seminars.

"I found, for example, that most of the people attending the session wanted more information on one phase of the subject than I had planned. Because I had good lecturers on hand, they were able to adjust and provide the information the people wanted. But the important thing is that this showed me I had to alter the curriculum a bit for future seminars."

It's important to do what Leonard did and conduct a prototype session before developing your final, long-range plans.

STEP SIX:
Guide Your Expansion

"After the first few sessions, the business almost guided its own growth and development," Leonard states. "Of course I made the decisions, but they were based on what I learned at the initial sessions. My wife, Roxy, and I often laugh at the fact that I was learning more at those early seminars than the customers were!"

Here's the type of thing you'll learn at your initial seminars, and which will be helpful in making your business grow as rapidly as possible:

- The course materials that appeal most to those who attend. (By giving this greater play in your advertising, you'll sign up more people.)
- How to pick the best available lecturers (if you are not going to do this yourself).
- The largest "class" size you should attempt to deal with, and how much space you should reserve.
- The type of advertising that gets the best results in your particular field.
- How frequently you can conduct your seminar in a given city.

"Even though I still had a lot to learn at the time of my first seminar, I had prepared well enough so that it returned a profit," Leonard says. "And it was enough money to pay for planning, scheduling, and conducting the next several seminars in other cities."

Leonard is now a full-time "seminarian." He sponsors scores of sessions in many different cities. His income is over $75,000 a year.

25 HIGHLY PROFITABLE TRAINING FIELDS

As with the seminar listings, many of the fields presented here are broad categories rather than individual subjects. To include each of the subjects would multiply the length of the listings many times.

Thus, the listing is "Foreign Languages" rather than "Spanish," "Russian," or "Mandarin Chinese." The list does give you an excellent idea about what is being profitably taught on a commercial basis in many communities throughout the land.

Most of the items listed are self-explanatory. In some cases, however, I offer some brief comments as to why the particular subject has proven successful as the basis of a commercially-operated training business.

Antiques: These are increasingly popular as investments or simply as collectors' items. Since intelligent investing and collecting requires specialized knowledge, many people are signing up for classes on this subject.

Dancing

Dieting: The same information is available in books and in magazine articles, but many people are more successful at losing weight when it's done as a group project—and when there's a group leader to keep them in line . . . or, to put it more fittingly, to get them in trim.

Dog Training: Again, people can learn this from a book, but interaction with other people and other dogs makes dog training classes so popular. It's fine to train your dog in your backyard if that's the only place he will ever be. But if you plan to take him out in public, he's got to learn how to behave when other creatures—canine and human—are around, and that's where group classes are helpful.

Drama: Breathes there a soul who does not fancy himself an actor upon the stage? Well, a few, I guess. But since so many people have a yen to act, drama classes taught by accomplished professionals do very well.

Driving

Flying

Foreign Languages

Golf

Hobby Skills: This category could probably be broken down into hundreds of individual hobby subjects. People who are fascinated with a particular hobby will go to great lengths—and pay considerable sums—to become expert at the craft involved.

Horsemanship

Investments: Once again, scores of subjects are available under this broad category. Commercial courses are being taught on everything from stocks and bonds to coins, raw land, diamonds, and much more.

Job Skills
Music
Oil Painting
Photography
Public Speaking
Sailing
Self Defense
Small Business Management
Speed Reading
Swimming
Tennis
Typing
Writing

HOW TO START AND RUN A BUSINESS BASED ON TRAINING

There are four basic factors to consider in setting up a business that involves teaching other people:

1. The subject
2. The instructor(s)
3. The location
4. The students

Let's see how you can make the right decisions in each of these four areas so that your enterprise can quickly start bringing in the kind of money you desire.

STEP ONE:
Choose Your Subject

The subject you select as the basis of your business should be one that:

- You are completely familiar with
- Newcomers are constantly seeking to learn
- Cannot be easily self-taught

These are the three criteria used by Clara H. in deciding to teach speed-reading courses. Years previously, she had taken a speed-reading course at a community college. She used the ability constantly in her work as the associate editor of a small weekly newspaper.

"I received hundreds of news releases in the mail each week and had to make quick decisions on which items to use and how to use them," she says. "I even developed some of my own speed-reading techniques that went beyond what I had learned in the course I had taken."

After she got married, Clara left her newspaper job but continued to use speed-reading in the books and magazine articles she read for personal enjoyment. After her children were grown, she began to think of it as a source of income.

"I knew that many people who had a lot of reading to do in their work were prime candidates for taking such a course," she says, "and while it was being taught in a local adult education program, I felt that what they were doing there did not go far enough—especially in light of the techniques I had developed on my own. True, books were available on the subject at the local library, but many people simply are not geared to self-study. They need the guidance of an instructor and interaction with other students."

Thus the criteria of (1) personal familiarity with the subject, (2) an abundance of potential students, and (3) its not being easily self-taught guided Clara to the subject that would be the basis of her business. These same criteria should be your guides.

STEP TWO:
Pick Your Instructors

"No problem there!" Clara asserts. "I was the instructor. No one else knew the precise method I planned to teach. And besides, I started on a small scale, with an initial class of about 15 students."

Regardless of your subject, you should do the same. By handling the instruction yourself at the start, you can sharpen your course so that it becomes of even greater value to the students. As Clara notes, "Only by teaching the class yourself can you discover the areas where students have the most difficulty and the areas where your planned teaching methods may not be entirely satisfactory."

But, naturally, as the number of your students and your classes grows, you can't continue to do all the teaching yourself. "Where," you ask, "can I find qualified instructors?"

The answer is simple! You'll find your future instructors from among the graduates of your own course. Many of the best-known training businesses in the nation follow this procedure, among them the Dale Carnegie Course, Smokenders, and Weight Watchers.

"What you do," Clara advises, "is single out a few of your best students. When the time comes to expand and you need instructors, invite these students to teach for you, following course outlines you have prepared for them. Most of the people I've invited to do this are really excited about it."

STEP THREE:
Find a Location

In some cases this is no problem at all. If, for example, you are teaching music, the instruction can be done in your own home or the home of the student. If you're teaching driving, then it's done on public roads. If the subject is sailing, it's done aboard your boat.

But if, as in Clara's case, you plan group classes, you'll need to "rent a hall," as they say. And this is easily and inexpensively accomplished. Because of the educational nature of your business, you'll find that many community organizations, churches, and even public schools are willing to rent space at a nominal fee.

"I started out by renting a church hall for $15 a night," Clara recalls. "It was centrally located, perfectly adequate, and worked out well."

The "problem"—if you want to call it that—comes after your business begins to grow and the number of class sessions increases.

"The time came," Clara continues, "when I simply had too many classes for the church hall to accommodate. After all, the church people had to use it some of the time! That's when I decided to rent a large office on a full-time basis."

The office contained two rooms: an outer reception area and a large inner room, where she held the actual classes. "This allowed me to have classes going day and night, five days a week," she states. Rather than offices, some people rent storefronts when they are available cheaply. But offices are generally obtainable at less cost than a first-floor storefront.

STEP FOUR:
Advertise for Students

Once you've chosen your subject, planned your instruction method, and found a location, the time comes to enroll students. How you do it depends on the subject being taught. Clara saw her subject as appealing mostly to (1) business and professional people who had a lot of reading to do, and (2) avid readers who wanted to devour the latest books and magazine articles at a much faster clip. She sought out these people by having an attractive brochure printed and sent to business and professional people listed in the area telephone directories, and to public libraries, many of which posted the brochure on their bulletin boards.

"Since the subject was of fairly general appeal, I also ran two ads in the local newspaper. These ads invited people to come in for a free 'trial' class. During that trial I demonstrated my method and showed them how I could read a piece of unfamiliar material in far less time than they could."

For most people who attended the free session, the clincher was the demonstration of Clara's own ability. They wanted to be able to do the same thing, and they readily signed up. This "free demonstration" is a common practice in most self-improvement type courses.

Here are some other ways to attract students:

- Notify clubs and organizations that are active in the field you plan to teach.
- Invite some local newspaper and radio publicity by saying that you are available for an interview on your teaching methods and how they can benefit people.
- If the subject is suitable, contact area business firms and convince them that your course can make their key employees more productive and more valuable.
- Place posters throughout the community.
- Hire teenagers to go to public functions attended by people who are interested in the subject; the students are paid to distribute your brochures by putting them under the windshield wipers of parked autos.

"I even set up a booth at a local shopping mall," Clara reports. "I paid the management $100 for the lobby space for a period of five days. I installed a display showing what we did in class and what the students learned. Either I or one of my instructors was there to answer questions and sign up students. It worked quite well, and I've rented the booth space each year since then."

Clara does very little teaching herself these days. Her graduates handle it for her, being paid on a "per class" basis. As you have gathered, it has become a full-time business. She cleared more than $34,000 last year, and she's now planning to open a branch in a community located about 25 miles away.

How much did it cost her to start her business?

"Under $250," she boasts. "A simple brochure, a couple of ads, some teaching materials, and rental of the hall. That was it." Pretty good for a business that continues to show great potential for growth. But then, low-investment high-potential businesses are what this book is all about.

8

Sales Outlets That Can Make You Rich

How would you like to be part of the highest-paying profession that doesn't require a college degree? A profession that pays even more than many professions that do require degrees? Then consider selling, even if you don't want to do the selling yourself.

The fact is that you can make more money in the selling profession by not selling. Confusing? Read on.

HOW $1,300 CREATES A MILLION-DOLLAR SALES EMPIRE

Lloyd F. does no selling, has no employees other than his wife, and yet earns more than $75,000 a year in sales. His business grosses more than a million dollars annually.

How does he do it? "I don't do anything except shuffle papers in my home office, handle some phone calls, and count the money," he boasts. If he's over-simplifying the situation, it's not by much. Lloyd deals in magazine subscriptions. His "salesmen" are members of non-profit organizations across the country.

"A lot of commercial outfits sell magazine subscriptions," Lloyd comments, "but it's a tough business because most of the publishers themselves sell to new subscribers at substantial discounts."

So when Lloyd formed his business he had several factors in mind:

1. The only way to make real money would be to sell subscriptions at full price, and the best way to get subscribers to pay the full price is to have them buy the subscriptions from a local organization conducting a fund-raising drive.
2. Since there were already a number of national companies offering subscription campaigns to non-profit organizations, Lloyd decided that he would have to offer what these companies were not offering—smaller, special interest magazines.
3. There are hundreds of smaller magazines which cater to people with special interests in the hobby, recreation, study, work, and athletic fields. Being small, these magazines have little money for self-promotion and welcome effective ways to increase their circulations.

"I contacted all the publishers I found listed in a directory at the local library," Lloyd reports. "My deal was this: I would have volunteers for charitable organizations across the country sell subscriptions at full price, and I would pay the publishers half of that amount. The balance was to be split up between me and the charitable groups."

A COST-SAVING DEAL

Most magazine revenue comes from advertising, but in order to gain advertising most consumer-type publications must have an audited list of paid subscribers. The auditors don't care whether the publisher actually received the cash, as long as the subscribers paid cash. Most magazines actually spend a great deal of money soliciting their paid subscribers. It often costs them more than they receive in subscription revenues, and that's why most of the publishers Lloyd contacted eagerly accepted his deal.

"My goal was to set up a fund-raising program that could be used by various non-profit groups across the country," Lloyd notes. "The first step was to print up an attractive sales circular outlining the more than 100 publications on my list. Then I had another brochure printed, this one outlining how the program worked and how it could make money for groups seeking to raise funds. I sent this one to organizations whose names and addresses were on a rented mailing list."

Printing the brochures cost about $350. Lloyd spent another $450 for postage and $150 for stationery and office supplies. Then he sat back and waited for the outcome.

"Within a month I had five groups signed up. It was a small but profitable beginning. I sent them the sales material that I had prepared, and a short time after that the orders were arriving at my home office ready for my wife to process."

Initial profits allowed Lloyd to have his literature printed in greater volume, and the business has grown steadily ever since.

CHOOSE YOUR OWN PROFIT LEVEL

Charity sales—using the same basic method employed by Lloyd F.—is one of the ten powerful sales plans contained in this chapter. Any of these sales plans can be operated on as small a scale as you choose, or allowed to grow as large as their high potential allows. Lloyd had big ambitions, with the entire country as his market. If you want to, you can run a similar business on a strictly local level. It's entirely up to you.

There are two types of sales plans in this chapter:

- You sell directly to the customer
- Other people do the selling for you

Everything else being equal, the second category can be more profitable because you earn a cut of everybody else's commission, and that can add up to a big bundle.

I'm sure you're wondering why I bother to list the direct selling plans. I do so because some of them offer unique opportunities with little competition. They can be extremely easy to handle, bringing in sizable profits for the effort involved. So please consider carefully all of the plans listed in this chapter.

"MIDDLEMAN" YOUR WAY TO WEALTH

No matter which type of sales plan you choose, you are a "middleman." You are getting products or services from one party and selling them to another. The difference between what the first party charges and what the second party pays is your cut. That cut can range from a few percentage points to—in some cases—an amount that is actually a multiple of what the first party charged.

As Lloyd did, you will start on a small scale, with an investment of under $1,500. How far you go depends not so much on the plan you choose as on your own ambition.

So let's get started. Read through each of the plans before deciding which is best for you. I can assure you that whichever plan you choose, it will be one of the most unique money-making methods you have ever encountered. Although each of the methods has been proven by others who are now making money with it, it's also the type of plan that many people never think of. So there's plenty of room on the ground floor for you.

PLAN #1:
CASH IN ON CHARITY SALES

Having read about the experience of Lloyd F., you already know how the charity sales plan works. But of course magazines are not the only product that can be sold this way. And you don't have to start by dealing with clubs and organizations in a distant community. You can deal with those right in your own area.

As an illustration of how a community-based charity sales plan can be launched, consider the experience of Pamela C.

"I had been looking through one of the business opportunity magazines," she said, "searching for a business I could conduct. Most of the ads and articles dealt with products to sell. I'm not a salesperson and never have been. But I did spot a lot of attractive items that could be purchased at low prices in wholesale lots. My problem: How could I sell them?"

And then the charity sales plan idea hit her. Why not select a product, or a line of products, and have a local organization handle the sales as a fund-raising project?

What Pam settled on was imprinted note paper—stationery with either a monogram or the customer's full name and address printed on the top. The company she bought the stationery from offered several different styles.

"I approached the head of a local church group," she explains, "and suggested that she have her members show stationery samples to their friends, explaining that the net proceeds would go to the church. The leader liked the idea, the members became willing workers, and everyone benefited."

Pam's profit on that first project came to $275. Her only work was in ordering the initial supply of samples and then placing individual orders as they were passed on to her. The orders totaled more than $1,830, and her cut amounted to 15%. The church group got 20%. Here's the breakdown:

Total sales:	$1834.00
Wholesale cost	1192.10
20% for church	366.80
15% for Pamela	275.10

Since that initial project, Pam has had dozens of others in and near her home town. She's found that many of the organizations become "repeat customers" and the sales campaign has become an annual event with them.

"For an effort that's very part-time," she reports, "I'm earning close to $10,000 a year." If she wanted to, she could multiply that figure by 20, 30, or even a hundred. She could do it by taking her sales program to other areas in addition to where she lives.

Charity Best-Sellers

Here are 30 items that can be easily sold by club volunteers as fund-raisers for their organizations. As a distributor to fund-raising groups, you can readily obtain these items on a wholesale basis. Examine ads in magazines such as *Specialty Salesman* and *Income Opportunities* for the names of manufacturers.

Address Labels	Golf and Tennis Balls
Appointment Books	Handbags
Art Reproductions	Knit Goods
Artificial Flowers	Light Bulbs
Belts	Magazine Subscriptions
Calculators	Memo Pads
Candles	Nuts
Candy	Recipe Books
Cheese	Shoes
Cosmetics	Spices
Costume Jewelry	Stationery
Cutlery	Towels
Decorative Items	Transistor Radios
Dinnerware	Wallets
Flashlights	Watchband Calendars

Here's a variation on charity sales you might want to consider: Sell products in bulk directly to members of clubs and organizations. Mel A., for example, gets himself invited to club meetings and then shows the members samples of his specially-molded candles, which can be produced with the club's emblem or motto molded in. He reports that at a typical club meeting he'll sell several hundred dollars worth.

"To assure that I'm invited back the next year," he says, "I always donate about 10% of the proceeds to the club treasury. There's more than enough profit to allow for this." So much profit, in fact, that Mel gave up a Civil Service job to go full-time into the specialty candle business.

PLAN #2:
BECOME A BROKER

You're aware of how the real estate broker operates, but did you know that brokers operate in many other fields as well? Many valuable items are sold through brokers, and with a commission ranging from 5% to 20%, there's a lot of money to be made this way. And since you are selling someone else's property, there's no requirement for an investment in inventory. All you need is a desk, a phone, and a file in which to keep your records. Many brokers operate out of their homes.

One such person is Morgan H., whose specialty is sailboats. Morgan lives in a yachting area on the East Coast. Knowing that boat owners often "upgrade" themselves by buying newer and larger craft, Morgan decided to get in on the action.

"When a sailboater decides he wants another boat," Morgan explains, "it can be a nuisance trying to sell the old one. Dealers won't give full retail value on a trade-in, so many owners try to sell privately. But that involves a lot of time—and that's where I come in. For 5% of the selling price, I'll show the boat to all interested parties. And I'm available weekdays when most sailboat owners are working and unavailable to show their craft."

The average sailboat that Morgan handles in his brokerage sells for $22,500. This provides him with a commission of $1125. "Many other brokers charge twice my 5% commission," Morgan reports, "but I actually make more money with the lower rate. That's because the seller usually jacks up his price to cover the commission he's going to have to pay. Thus, with my lower commission, I can offer boats at more attractive prices—and I sell more."

Morgan runs regular ads in the local newspapers and in the regional boating publications offering his services as a broker and including some of his current listings. When prospective buyers call him on the phone, he makes an appointment to meet them at the particular dock where the boat is berthed.

"Since about one out of every ten 'lookers' becomes a buyer, and since my average commission is $1125, I earn $112.50 every time I spend an hour or two to show people through a boat," he reports.

Choose a Field You Know

Do you have to be an expert to be a successful broker? Not at the start, most brokers tell me, but you should be familiar with the field. There's nothing worse for a prospective buyer than to have to deal with a salesman who doesn't know much about the product he's trying to sell.

That's why you should pick a field you know—one related to a hobby of yours, or related to your work experience. Do this, and although you may not be an "expert" at the start, you'll become one soon enough. That's because your beginning familiarity with the field, combined with the knowledge you gain in running your business week in and week out, will provide you with expertise no book could provide.

Getting yourself established as a broker can be as easy as choosing a field you know something about and then arming yourself with a business phone listing, some advertising, some business cards, and a car. Here are some examples of what is being done:

- *Business Brokerage.* A woman in California keeps in constant touch with the businesses in her community, inquiring about which shops are for sale. Many merchants who are capable behind the counter are not very good salesmen when it comes to selling their businesses. She handles these details for them and receives a 5% commission.

- *Art Brokerage.* There are big-time art brokers and small-time art brokers. A woman in Ohio is a small-time art broker when it comes to the names of the artists she deals with, but not when it comes to the money she makes. She handles the work of talented, aspiring artists who have not yet made the big leagues. She sells their work mainly to interior decorators, restaurateurs, building managers, and others who want medium-priced art to hang on their walls. The work is far superior to the mass-production art that is available in department stores, and it sells very well.

- *Real Estate.* A Vermont couple spotted a "Business Opportunity" ad seeking local agents for a national real estate brokerage firm. They opened an office in their home, with the national firm's sign out front. Its nationwide advertising helped them to obtain listings and buyers, and in their first year they handled gross sales totaling more than $200,000. Meanwhile, both husband and wife were studying for their own brokers' licenses, and in their third year in business they severed ties with the national firm and started doing business independently, thus getting to keep the entire commission in each sale.

There are a number of other fields in which a brokerage-type business can be launched at little expense, provided you have some experience in working with the type of product that is being sold. These include old coins, literary work, diamonds, antiques, rare stamps, private and corporate aircraft, and rare books. Remember that the high value of the items you sell has little or no bearing on the cost of setting up a brokerage because you are serving as an agent; you do not personally invest in any of the items in which you deal.

PLAN #3:
PROFIT FROM A PARTY PLAN

Many women have conducted sales parties in their homes and have made some money doing so, but a lot more money can be made by signing up other people to conduct the parties for you. Think about it for a moment. If you conduct one party, the only thing you can profit from is that one party. But if you have several—perhaps dozens—of parties going at the same time, you get a slice of each, and you can have all kinds of dollars rolling in.

Helen T. began as a traditional party plan operator, selling kitchenware to her friends. She was successful at it, but a conversation with the representative of the company that supplied her products brought a big change to her life.

"He had stopped by at one of my parties to help demonstrate the products and he happened to mention that he had four more such parties to attend that week," she recalls. "I joked that it must be painful to have to spend your time helping other people make money. He smiled for a moment and then acknowledged that the better they did financially, the better he did, because his company paid him on the basis of the total sales in his territory, which was the entire state."

In the next few weeks Helen did a lot of thinking about it, and she finally came to the conclusion that she could do even better than the man with whom she'd been speaking. After all, he was working for the national distributor, and they were getting a big slice of the pie, too. What if she were to set up her own little company, buying products directly from the manufacturer and distributing them directly to the home party-givers? With fewer people cutting into the pie, there'd be a giant piece left for her.

How to Set Up a Party Plan Business

There are two basic steps involved in establishing yourself as a regional (and eventually national?) party plan distributor:

1. Line up some products in a related field such as housewares or cosmetics.

2. Enlist women to demonstrate and take orders for these products in their homes.

To accomplish the first step, Helen went to the library and looked up the names and addresses of a number of trade magazines in the housewares, cosmetics, gift, and jewelry fields. She subscribed to several of the publications and finally settled on kitchenware because that was the field in which she'd had some party plan experience. She then wrote to a number of manufacturers and lined up several that would drop-ship products to the homes of customers.

Drop-shipping is an expression you won't find in most dictionaries, but it's a common business practice. It occurs when manufacturers agree to handle the orders of another business firm and then ship the product directly to the home of the person who bought the product from the second firm.

To accomplish the second step, Helen gave a party. It was similar to the parties she'd conducted in her home as a product salesperson— but this time Helen was enlisting other salespeople.

"I ran a classified ad in several local newspapers, seeking women who were interested in conducting kitchenware parties in their homes. Those who responded to the ad were invited to my home on the night of the party I had planned."

And when they arrived, the first part of the evening was much like any other product party—a demonstration of the items for sale. But the second part of the evening was different. Instead of the usual sales pitch, Helen explained to the women how they could make money selling these products in their own homes.

"About half of them agreed to give it a try," she reports, "and my business was happily launched."

After several months of successful operation in her own area, Helen expanded her business to another section of the state. This time she enlisted her salespeople by conducting a party in a rented motel meeting room. She's followed this same method in various communities over a broad territory.

"I began the business with an investment of about $500 for sample products and incidental supplies," she notes, "and now I'm clearing more than that each week. It certainly beats conducting little sales parties in my home, when the most I made was $30-$40 an evening and, because of my limited circle of acquaintances, could only give two or three parties a year."

What kind of product can be successfully sold via party plans? Consider this list:

Apparel	Gourmet Food Items
Art Reproductions	Health Foods
Books	Jewelry
Candies	Kitchenware
Candles	Novelties
Cosmetics	Personalized Items
Do-it-Yourself Kits	Plants
Figurines	Sewing Supplies
Gifts	Shoes

This is not a complete list, but it is representative of the items that sell well at home parties. Perusing this list plus the items you see advertised in trade and gift magazines should help you settle on the type of product line that can be the basis for your own successful party-sales business.

PLAN #4:
BECOME A DROP-SHIPPER

The businesses that most frequently use drop-shipping are mail order firms. They find it easier to offer items they don't have to hold in stock than to maintain a large inventory of items. Usually, drop-shippers are the companies that manufacture the items, but not always.

Sherwin A. is a drop-shipper who is not a manufacturer. He supplies small mail order firms with products that they can list in their catalogs. He buys his products from manufacturers, tags on a profit for himself, and then, as the orders come in, he ships the products directly to the customers who placed the order from the mail order firm.

"Many people start small mail order operations from their homes," Sherwin explains, "and these are the people I cater to. They don't have room to stock all the items they offer, so they look for drop-shippers to deal with. As they receive the orders, they send the information on to the drop-shipper along with their own mailing label. This makes it appear that the item came directly from them."

There are several advantages to being a drop-shipper, the principal of which is that you avoid what is usually the biggest expense in mail order: the consumer advertising.

"I run inexpensive ads in the 'Business Opportunities' section of several national magazines," Sherwin explains. "These ads let the small mail order operators know about my drop-shipping arrangement. That's my only advertising. Thus I am able to sell a lot of products through a lot of individual dealers at almost no advertising expense."

What kind of product can be sold with the drop-shipping arrangement? Go back to Chapter 6 and examine the list of 50 proven mail order specialties. Almost any item mentioned there can be drop-shipped.

PLAN #5:
BE A FLEA MARKET ORGANIZER

The lure here is similar to that of party plans: It's profitable to be a flea market dealer, but it's more profitable to be a flea market organizer.

If you're at all familiar with flea markets, you know that they consist of dozens, or perhaps hundreds, of tables and stalls set up by individuals who pay anywhere from $4 to $20 for their booth space. They are attended by hundreds or even thousands of people looking for bargains. Some of the individual dealers make several hundred dollars a day; others break even or occasionally lose a bit. But the flea market organizer, the one who knows what he or she is doing, almost never loses.

How do you learn the flea market business? By doing two things:

1. Attend all the flea markets that you can, until you become thoroughly familiar with how they operate.
2. Gain some experience as a dealer at flea markets so that you learn the "inside" workings of the business.

Once you have gone through these two training steps you'll be prepared to set yourself up as an organizer. It can be done by:

1. Renting a large open space or hall.
2. Announcing your coming event a month or two in advance, placing ads in the papers read by flea market "addicts"—both sellers and attendees.
3. Hiring two or three people to help you manage the event on the weekend during which it is held.

Maurice K. went into the flea market business after being a dealer for about six months. "I sold surplus goods that I found through manufacturers' closeout ads in the paper. I often made $500 on a weekend as a dealer," he notes. "But now I conduct a flea market once a month in a community college field house that I rent. And I generally clear $5,000 per event." The money comes from (1) stall fees paid by the dealers, and (2) the admission charge paid by the shoppers who go to browse.

PLAN #6:
MANAGE GARAGE SALES

Garage sales are popular in America, and they could be even bigger if they were run correctly. But most of them are not, and thus at the end of a typical weekend you can stop by at any of a thousand garage sales and find a lot of items remaining unsold.

This is because the people who conduct garage sales are not professionals. They don't know what to charge, how to bargain, how to advertise, and in general, how to "move the merchandise."

That's where you can come in—as a garage sale organizer. Naturally, you need a working familiarity with garage sales and the value of items being sold (a few reference books will help here), and a willingness to give up your weekends in order to make money.

By serving as an advisor and organizer for families who wish to conduct garage or yard sales, you can increase their profits and earn 15% of what they take in.

That's precisely what Margaret S. does. And just to cover herself, she imposes a $50 minimum fee. "That's merely to protect me in the event that the owner insists on tagging the items with ridiculously high prices despite my advice not to do it," she explains.

That, it seems, is the trouble with most garage sales. The people simply have inflated ideas about what their items are worth. Margaret comments, "They remember what they paid for the goods in the store, and they imagine that the things have held a lot of their value. Of course, people go to garage sales to get bargains, and when they don't find them they leave empty-handed."

So when Margaret is retained as a garage sale organizer, the first thing she does after looking at the items to be offered is advise the owner on what the realistic prices would be. When, as often happens, the owner is surprised, she explains that there are two alternatives: set unrealistically high prices and sell only a few things, or set fair prices and have nearly everything sold.

And Margaret makes an offer that is hard to refuse. "I tell them that if they allow me to set the prices, I will personally buy anything that is left over at the end of the day, paying 70% of the tagged price. In other words, they are assured that everything will sell for at least 70% of the asking price, and most items will sell at full price."

What does Margaret do with the leftovers she takes as part of the agreement? "I consign them to a local auction house. The auctioneer charges me 20% commission. Usually the items sell for a bit more than the original tagged price (auction prices are generally higher than realistic garage sale prices), so I break even or make a small profit."

The purpose of removing the leftovers is not to make a profit, but to provide a service that no other garage sale organizers in her area are providing. This gives her the bulk of the business—and a profitable business it is. Margaret manages an average of ten garage sales a month, and she has reached the point where she can be choosy about the ones she agrees to handle. Her net profit amounts to $750 a month for work that is far from full-time.

Margaret built her business by advertising in the same classified newspaper columns where people planning garage sales advertised. Now, though, she does no advertising other than to place a small poster at each garage sale she organizes.

"The people see how well organized and efficient it is, and many of them ask me to do the same for them."

PLAN #7:
PROFIT FROM AN INFO-PHONE

Your telephone, working alongside an inexpensive answering machine, can be the basis of a highly lucrative business providing information that people are anxious to receive. Your income comes from commercials that are played over the phone along with the recorded information.

The information-phone concept is so popular that even the telephone company is getting into the act. In a number of major metropolitan areas special numbers have been set aside that people can call to hear the latest news, get some gardening tips, listen to the joke of the day, or learn their horoscope. Except for its long-established weather forecasts, Ma Bell started cashing in on the information type of service only after it noticed all the money that was being made by independent info-phone companies.

It's far from too late for you to get into the act. In areas where info-phone services already exist, you won't want to duplicate what's already being offered, but there are enough varieties of this service to make room for you no matter where you live.

Let's examine a typical info-phone service and see how it operates. Let's say that Mary Smith wants to know whether or not to send Johnny to school with his raincoat. It isn't raining now, but she thinks it might in the afternoon. Her local radio station doesn't give the forecast frequently enough, and it costs a dime or so to call the telephone company's weather number.

So Mary calls her town's info-phone service, and this is what she hears:

> *Good morning, this is the Riverview Weather Phone. Today's forecast is brought to you by the Harrison Smith Company, Riverview's leading department store. Today's specials at Harrison Smith include women's shoes at half-price. That's right! Yesterday's prices have been cut in half on a fine selection of ladies' footwear in up-to-the-minute styles. In fact, for low prices every day of the year, make a habit of shopping at Harrison Smith. And now the forecast for Riverview and vicinity. Cloudy this morning, but with the sun breaking through by noon, with a bright, sunny, and warm afternoon, high in the 70's. Tonight, mild, low in the 60's. Tomorrow, sunny and warm, high temperature in the 70's again. This forecast, brought to you by Harrison Smith Company, will be updated at noon. Thanks for calling Weatherphone.*

Mary Smith now has the information she needs. She won't send a raincoat along with Johnny when he trudges off to school. The brief commercial was little enough to "pay" for obtaining the information she needed, at the moment she wanted it.

What does it take to start an info-phone service? You can start with a single phone and a single answering machine, adding phones as the number of callers and advertisers warrants. The only other requirement is that you somehow let people know the type of information you are providing, and the number they can call.

How $350 Launches a Money-Maker

Ben G. started a weatherphone service in his community for $350, and his advertising revenues now exceed $200 a week. Ben began by inserting some small ads in the local newspaper announcing the service and listing the number, and also by hanging some posters at strategic locations in town. Of course he did not, at first, have enough callers to warrant the sale of advertising, so he used the time that would normally be allotted for this to run some plugs for his own business—inviting businesses to buy commercial "spots" on the info-phone tapes.

A few calls to local business establishments also helped to convince his initial sponsors that they should sign up. And before long his phone forecasts were "sold out." Keeping track of the number of phone calls received, he soon found it appropriate to add two more phones and recording machines.

Ben works a regular job, and the actual forecasts and commercials are recorded by his wife during the hours when he is away from home. She gets the basic information by calling the regular phone company weather number and jotting down the forecast. Then she types it up and reads it into the phone answering machines.

Many different kinds of information can be offered on info-phones and then "sold" to advertisers:

Community Calendar	Marine and Aviation Forecasts
Farm Prices	Regional Sports News
Horoscopes	School Closings
Items to Swap	Ski Reports
Local News	Stock Prices
Lost and Found	Weather

Some info-phone companies offer more than one type of information, especially when what they offer is needed at only certain times of the day. A company in New Jersey, for example, provides school closing information in the morning, runs an "items to swap" feature during mid-day, and relays stock prices throughout the afternoon and early evening. This way the phones are kept occupied throughout the day and different categories of listeners and sponsors are attracted.

PLAN #8:
TRY THE TRADE SHOWS

You've got a captive audience when you sell merchandise or services at trade shows. People have paid to get in, a large crowd passes your booth, and because trade shows are specialized in nature, you know that the people are interested in what you have to sell.

Rose P. rents booth space at hobby and craft shows throughout the country. Her product is how-to books. People attending such shows are looking to buy crafts materials and to obtain crafts information. They are prime prospects for the instructional volumes that she displays.

"Most book publishers offer a 40% discount to dealers," she explains, "and since the average book I sell goes for $10, I'm making a gross profit of $4 on each volume." Selling more than 100 books a day gives her a clear profit of better than $250 after all expenses have been deducted.

Visit any trade show and you'll see a variety of items being offered—all tied in with the theme of the show. Most booths are rented by full-time companies in the field. At a regional boat show, for example, space is rented mostly by boat dealers, boating magazines, and boating supply stores. But look closely and you'll see some part-timers there as well, selling items that may or may not be directly related to boating.

Eric Y. is typical of the part-timer who makes excellent money by attending shows of various types. He sells a product that can fit in at many different shows. It is a rustic-styled name sign, with the owner's name engraved on a piece of rough wood with jagged edges. This sign is sold at boat shows for use as boat nameplates; at home shows for installation on front lawns; at hunting and camping shows for use at vacation and hunting cabins; at recreational vehicle shows for installation on trailers and motor homes; and at motel-owners conventions, where they are ordered as signs to identify the various buildings and rooms in a motel complex.

Eric displays a variety of sign styles in his booth and then takes orders. The actual work is done by a company he has contracted with. The signs are generally on their way to the customer within three days of the show at which the order was placed.

How to Pick Your Trade Show Product

Want to know how you can get scores of ideas to consider? You can get those ideas by, you guessed it, attending the next several trade shows that come your way. Examine all the booths carefully. See how others handle their merchandise, listen to the sales pitches that are presented, and look for item types that fit into more than one highly specialized type of show. If you can find such an item (and if you keep at it, you will), then go home and locate supply sources.

How do you learn when and where trade shows are conducted? By reading the trade journals. Some are available at your local library, but others will have to be ordered. Their names and addresses are listed in directories, which are also available at the library.

PLAN #9:
SELL FROM A TRAVELING BOOTH

Similar in nature to the trade show plan, the idea presented here also deals with a booth that you set up in rented space to use in selling special interest products. Instead of attending trade shows, however, you go to shopping malls.

You've undoubtedly seen temporary booths installed in shopping mall lobbies. They sell such products and services as:

Art Reproductions	Horoscopes
Candies	Nameplates
Candles	Novelties
Charcoal Portraits	Oil Paintings
Computer-Printed Portraits	Old Coins and Stamps
Decorated T-Shirts	Plants
Electronic Organs	Seeds

These are, of course, just a few of the items being sold in shopping mall booths set up by traveling merchants, many of whom operate their businesses as part-time enterprises. Many malls are willing to rent such space for a day, a weekend, or a week at a time, provided that one vital rule is met: The products must not be in direct competition with what full-time merchants at the mall are already selling.

Thus, if there is a music store in the mall selling organs, you would not be allowed to set up a booth selling the same thing. But when no direct competition is involved, merchants and mall owners welcome such booths because they help attract shoppers.

PLAN #10:
BE AN AUCTIONEER

When people move to smaller quarters, or in cases of divorce or death, a lot of furniture and household goods have to be disposed of, and there is usually too much for a garage sale. As an auctioneer, you can solve their problem and make good money for yourself—as much as several thousand dollars per auction.

Warren R. entered the auction business after volunteering to conduct a charity auction for a local organization. It went so well and he enjoyed it so much that he decided to try a commercial auction of his own. He ran an ad in the local newspaper's classified column seeking household items and antiques on consignment. This meant that people seeking to dispose of such things would agree to let them go to the highest bidder, and to pay Warren a 25% commission.

For his first auction, Warren rented a church hall. It cost him $25. He hired some teenagers to lug heavy items during the sale, and this cost $65. He ran some display ads in the paper and circulated some auction posters; the advertising cost came to $175. Incidental expenses were $35, bringing the grand total to $300.

"I sold $4500 worth of merchandise in that first auction," Warren recalls. "My commission came to $1125. Deduct from that the $300 in expenses, and I had a clear profit of $825. Not bad for the first time out as a professional!"

The good thing about this profitable business is that it can be run entirely on evenings and weekends. Warren was an executive with a firm located in a nearby city. "I find auctioneering recreational as well as profitable," he says. "It's entirely different from the regular work I did, and this was relaxing."

Prior to each auction he spends several evenings at the hall he has rented accepting deliveries of consigned goods brought in by the sellers. He organizes the merchandise the night before the sale, which is always held on a Saturday when people are home from work and available to attend auctions.

Most of his advertising is now done by means of a mailing list he has developed by having people who attend sales sign a sheet with their names and addresses if they want to be notified of forthcoming auctions.

Get Higher Prices

Occasionally he avoids having to pay rent at all. This is when entire household lots are to be sold, in which case he conducts the sale directly from the yard of the home from which the goods are coming. "I get higher prices at house auctions," Warren notes. "People who attend auctions tend to bid to a higher level when they see goods coming out of a home. So I get extra profit two ways: not having to pay rent, and earning bigger commissions due to the higher prices."

Can you become an auctioneer? You can if you:

- Have a gift for gab
- Have evenings and weekends free
- Have a station wagon or pickup truck

- Can obtain whatever local license may be needed
- Have an interest in secondhand merchandise, be it antique or just plain "junque"

"A lot of people never think of becoming an auctioneer because they have a false notion that fast-talking is needed," Warren comments. "They've seen tobacco or cattle auctioneers on TV, talking 50 kilometers a minute . . . so fast, in fact, that most people can't understand them. You don't talk that way at merchandise auctions. You speak understandably. The only requirement is that you move the items along at a good clip, not dawdling over any one particular thing."

Since just about any fair-sized community can support a part-time auction business, this just might be the sales plan you've been looking for. By attending some auctions conducted by others, you'll get a feel for the business and soon recognize whether it's something you'd like to do as a money-making project. And money-making it will be if there's not much local competition and if you work hard (at first) to develop your mailing list and your reputation as an auctioneer.

"It's largely a word-of-mouth business," Warren explains, "with one auction fan telling another about upcoming sales. And soon some of the people who attend the auctions will be bringing things for you to sell on their behalf. And occasionally one of them will steer you to a really lucrative house auction."

Warren is retired from his job now, and he's earning just as much from his part-time auction enterprise as he did during the peak of his "working" career.

"I wish," he says, "that I had retired a lot sooner."

9

Be a Part-Time Publisher

All of the money-makers you will learn about in this chapter have one common theme: compiling and selling information. The market for information, especially the 38 types mentioned here, has never been greater. We'll be talking about how you can put that information in saleable form at minimum cost—and then demand top dollar for what you've done. The markup will be much greater than for most other things you can sell. The man who sells a pair of shoes may have marked up his cost by 30% or 40%, but with information it is not unusual to get double or triple your cost from the customer.

HOW $1,400 LEADS TO $150,000 A YEAR

Walter S. was a union shop steward in a manufacturing plant until one day when he lost a bid for reelection.

"That meant," Walter explains, "that if I wanted to keep on getting paid, I'd have to go back to the production line, attaching the same washers and nuts to the same bolts eight hours a day every day of the work week. Fortunately for me, that's not what I wanted to do."

It was fortunate for Walt because he decided instead to start his own business based on the subject he knows best—labor relations. He launched a newsletter that is sold to more than 5,000 subscribers who pay $50 a year to receive the four-page publication.

"That may sound like a lot of money to pay for a four-page letter that's typed in my office and then run off in a print shop," Walt notes, "but the subscribers badly need the type of information that I provide. The proof that it's worth every dollar I charge is the fact that more than 75% of the subscribers renew their subscriptions each year."

Walt's publication is written for the people who used to be on the "other side of the fence" from him—the employers whose workers have union contracts. These employers want to be kept abreast of the latest laws affecting their hiring and employment practices, they want to know the techniques used by other employers in conducting contract negotiations, and they want to know the effective incentive techniques being used to spur employee production.

Walt chose this as the subject of his first newsletter because he had worked in labor relations and knew it well. Now, after several years of publishing, he knows it a lot better because a lot of his time is spent scanning business and trade magazines, other newsletters, and several large newspapers, clipping appropriate items.

"That's what most newsletters consist of," Walt says. "They compact reams of published material down to four or six pages that busy executives can read in a few minutes. The executives thus get all the 'meaty' news they seek without having to spend hours searching for the exact material they want."

You'll note that I referred to this as Walt's first newsletter. He now has six, published in a variety of fields. The success of his first venture tipped him off to the big money that can be made by providing busy executives with a digest of the news they need to know to do their jobs more effectively.

Walt started the business that now earns $150,000 a year with an investment of $1,400. I'm sure you'd like to know how he got it started—and how you might be able to enter this lucrative field.

NEWSLETTERS: TODAY'S EASIEST PUBLISHING FIELD

Here's why newsletters are so inexpensive to launch:

- They are printed inexpensively
- They are distributed in low volume
- They can be started by one person working alone
- Finding subscribers is easier because the newsletter is aimed at one highly specialized audience

Let's see how Walt took advantage of each of these benefits to set up his high-profit publishing empire.

- *Inexpensive to Print.* Except for the masthead on the top of the first page, there usually is little or no typesetting involved in newsletter production. The material is typed on a regular typewriter and then taken to a print shop for reproduction. Even the printed masthead is a low-cost item because it is a one-time expense. It only has to be set in type once; newsletters are reproduced by the photo offset method and thus anything on paper (including the original masthead) can be accurately and cheaply reproduced.

- *Low-Volume Distribution.* Newspapers and general circulation magazines depend on high circulations to exist. They need a lot of readers in order to get advertisers. Newsletters carry no advertisements; their income is derived from the subscribers alone. And because they are aimed at a small, select audience which pays top dollar, they do not have the production and subscription sales expenses encountered by most other types of publications.

- *One-Person Operations.* Monthly newsletters do not need a sizable staff because they deal with one subject field. One person who is knowledgeable in the field can handle the entire job alone, especially if he or she has the printing of the publication and its related sales letters handled by an outside shop. Walt, for example, typed his own newsletter and then took it to a nearby quick print shop that reproduced the material at minimal cost. As he added other newsletters to his "stable" he hired a secretary to handle correspondence and subscription fulfillment for him, and then he engaged a young man to serve as editor of the various publications.

- *Easily-Found Subscribers.* Walt obtained his first subscriptions by renting a mailing list of the names of labor relations managers of large firms across the United States. Later he rented lists of company presidents, government agencies, and even union officials, with almost equal success in each category. He employed "pinpoint" advertising—getting the word out to the very people who would be most interested in subscribing to his publication, and only those people. He got a much higher ratio of subscription orders than do general circulation publications that must send their subscription sales letters to the public at large.

Of course, business newsletters comprise just one of the publishing fields we're discussing in this chapter. Now let's take a look at the entire list of 38 businesses you can launch at low cost with high-profit opportunities.

38 PUBLISHING BUSINESSES YOU CAN START FROM SCRATCH

As you examine this list, pay particular attention to the subjects that are related to your own personal interests, work experience, or hobbies. You'll note that nearly all of the categories in the list deal with serving the special interests of others; if you pick a field where you share those interests, you'll be able to do a better and more profitable job right at the outset.

Boat Directory: If you live in a region where a lot of people are actively involved in boating, issuing a periodic boat directory could be the publishing field for you. A boat directory is a classified ad-type publication where people advertise used boats for sale. Such directories have proven more effective than newspaper classified columns because they contain hundreds of listings all in the same field. They're placed at newsstands and on magazine racks, with the distribution handled by the same local or regional agency that places magazines and paperback books at those locations.

Business Field Newsletter: You've read of the success achieved by Walter S., but perhaps you don't know that there are hundreds of other people like him across the United States who have achieved similar success in the newsletter field by catering to specialized business interests. You can learn about these people and what they are doing by subscribing to *The Newsletter on Newsletters.* Write to the Newsletter Clearinghouse, 44 West Market St., Rhinebeck, N.Y. 12572 for information on how to subscribe to this helpful publication.

Classified Ad Paper: This is similar to the boat directory described above, except that it contains many classifications ranging from "Household Articles" to "Help Wanted." It is usually distributed free to all households in a given area. In the area where I live, for example, I have found that ads placed in the local "Pennysaver" bring far better results than those in the daily newspaper's classified ad column. Youngsters are hired to drop it off at each home in their neighborhoods.

Commercial Brochures: Your specialty here is coordinating

the work involved in printing sales brochures for other business firms. A client comes to you with the information he wants reproduced and you take it to the appropriate people: a typesetter, a layout specialist, a commercial artist, whoever is needed to perform the various tasks involved. Then you take it to the printer who can do the best work for the particular job. Your cut is about 15% of what the various specialists charge. It's worth it to the client because he gets a much more professional-looking brochure than would be possible if he attempted to arrange it all himself.

Company Publications: Many large firms issue "house organs" for distribution to their employees and perhaps to their customers as well. In many cases they don't have the staff to handle the editing and production themselves, so they hire the work to be done on the "outside." That's where you can come in—writing, editing, and arranging for the printing of company house organs. You get the information that's to be included from the company and then put it in printed form ready for distribution to the firm's employees and customers.

Compiled Mailing List: Having read Chapter 6, you know how much mail order firms depend on mailing lists. You can make money by meeting this important need, compiling lists of names of people in various categories. This is considered "publishing" under the terms we're using in this chapter because you are doing what any other publisher does—you are compiling information, having it reproduced on paper, and then selling it to interested parties. There are thousands of categories to choose from for compiling mailing lists. You obtain the information from such sources as phone books, trade publications, and organization membership lists.

Construction Plans: Do-it-yourselfers are prime prospects to buy plans for carrying out various projects they are interested in. The person who builds his own home buys construction plans; so do the people who want to build furniture, electronic devices, light airplanes, campers, boats, hunting cabins, home additions, patios, and any of a thousand other things. Once the plans are drawn and the instructions written, the reproduction cost is small. Something that costs you less than a dollar to print can sell for $50 or more. You sell the plans by running small ads in special interest magazines.

Controlled Circulation Magazine: There's hardly a business firm in America that doesn't receive at least one controlled circulation magazine—a publication it didn't ask for and doesn't pay for. Yet these free magazines are read because they deal specifically with the type of business in which the recipients are engaged. They earn their income from advertising. The advertisers are companies that offer products and services geared to the particular industry served by the magazine. It's a highly effective advertising medium. How can you get started with less than $1,500 of your own money? By lining up advertisers and then borrowing the cash needed to print your first issue, using the money due you from the advertisers as collateral.

Disc Jockey Patter: Do you think all the jokes and informational tidbits meted out by disc jockeys each day are original? Think again. A lot of it is material that they bought. If you can think up a number of topical one-liners each month, you may have the basis for a successful publishing business. Check a copy of the latest *Broadcasting Yearbook* at your local library and send a sample copy of your patter to the stations listed in that directory. Or, if you don't want to lick a lot of stamps and envelopes to send out material on speculation to all those thousands of stations, insert a small ad in the weekly trade magazine issued by the same company. It's called simply *Broadcasting*. Check other ads that appear each week near the back of the magazine for style and content.

Dress Patterns: These are prepared and sold in much the same way as you would handle construction plans, listed earlier. The major difference is that dress patterns go for considerably less money than do most construction plans, so you must sell them in higher volume. They're usually sold through display ads in magazines, but I know of one enterprising individual who is making $40,000 a year part-time by running a pattern-of-the-month club, operated much like a book club.

Flea Market Calendar: A monthly or bi-monthly publication listing all of the flea markets in a particular state or region can appeal to thousands of flea market addicts. Most of the revenue will have to come from subscription and single copy sales, although this can be augmented by money received from display advertising by some of the larger flea market operators. Single copy sales are accomplished by having the publication distributed to news-stands by the regional magazine distributor; each issue should contain an order form so that interested readers can enter subscriptions to receive it monthly in the mail.

Hobbyist Newsletter: The theme here is providing specific information about a hobby or hobby product, giving the reader more accurate information than he or she can obtain elsewhere. One of the main selling points of such newsletters is that since they contain no advertising, they can afford to be totally independent in what they say about various products. They have to be low in price because they are sold to individuals, not to business firms that can write off the expense. An example is the personal computer hobby. There are a number of newsletters in this field, each geared to owners or potential owners of a particular brand. Since the newsletters are published by people not associated with the particular manufacturer, they can contain information the manufacturer would never disclose on its own.

How-To Books: Instructional books, the kind that teach people how to acquire a new skill, are among the most saleable on the market today. You can get started in this field by writing and publishing a how-to booklet and using the profits from that project to issue more booklets, gradually increasing the size of your volumes until they reach full-sized book status. You'll see an example of how this was done later in the chapter.

Idea Letter: Not all newsletters are based on news. Some center on ideas that a subscriber can use profitably in his business or profession. Businesses are constantly looking for new ways to get the public's attention through advertising; investors and promoters are searching for new kinds of business enterprises they can launch; producers are looking for new and different kinds of entertainment they can sponsor; editors desire ideas for unique articles. Fresh ideas play an important role in the success of virtually every activity, and that's why idea newsletters are so successful.

Instructional Portfolios: This type of publishing is similar to the first phase of issuing how-to books. The difference here is that you continue to concentrate on booklets or portfolios instead of graduating to full-fledged, hard-cover books. As your business grows, you develop a growing line of instructional booklets, eventually having a full catalog of selections to offer customers. The publications are sold via small classified and display ads in national magazines.

Investment Letter: There are hundreds of these, and most of them seem to be making good money. They offer stock market advice based on a particular investment theory that the publisher or editor believes to be effective. In order to dispense investment advice you must be registered with the federal government as an investment advisor. This is easy to accomplish. All you do is fill out a form and send it on to Washington.

Local Phone Book: In areas where the local phone book covers many communities, forcing you to wade through a lot of Smiths before you find the Smith you want, independently-published, really local phone books can be a blessing. Getting the data is easy; all you do is extract all the listings for a particular town from the larger phone book put out by Ma Bell. Your income is derived from advertisements that can be placed at the top and bottom of each page and on the covers.

Local Recipes: This is a fund-raising project for church, PTA, and other non-profit groups. Volunteers collect the favorite recipes of many of the organization's members and you publish them in booklet form, with the organization purchasing the booklets from you for a price agreed upon in advance. Your profit is the difference between what it costs you to print the booklets and what the organization pays you. Start by working with just one organization to gain experience and additional capital, and gradually expand your activities. Eventually, you can be publishing such booklets for hundreds of groups each year.

Locally Prominent People: Nearly everyone likes to see his name in print, and an even more welcome sight is a published write-up of a person's background and accomplishments. That's why a local imitation of the well known *Who's Who* book can be financially successful. List a thousand people who have achieved some sort of local or regional prominence and you should be able to sell a thousand copies. (Not all who are mentioned will buy, but multiple purchases, plus sales to libraries, etc. will make up the difference.) Charge $10 per copy and half of the $10,000 you receive should be profit. Success in one region will enable you to achieve similar success elsewhere and do it more efficiently on the basis of the experience you've gained.

Looseleaf Guides with Update: One of the drawbacks of most types of books is that they are permanent; a new edition must be published before the information can be brought up to date. Thus, business and tax information is often published in looseleaf form. When there is data that needs to be changed, all the publisher has to do is print and insert a corrected page; hardly any bother or expense at all. But a greater advantage—and a distinct selling point—is the possibility of selling a subscription along with the looseleaf publication. The customer buys the original book and then pays an additional fee for periodic inserts that guarantee that the information will be current. Most looseleaf-with-update publications deal with "how-to" topics such as saving on taxes, running a particular type of business, increasing sales, handling personnel problems, making successful investments, etc. An example is given later in the chapter.

Municipal Contract Bulletin: There are many businesspeople whose livelihoods depend on municipal contracts. These are the people who supply cars and trucks to municipal agencies, build city halls, sell salt for the roads, and provide the various goods and services that every municipality needs. The law in most areas provides that such purchases must be put out for bid, enabling all interested business firms to get a crack at the contract. By keeping track of what bids are being sought and by which agency, you can issue a bulletin that would be of tremendous value to people seeking such contracts.

Professional Newsletter: Just as businessmen depend on newsletters like those published by Walter S., professional people also need to keep up on the latest developments in their career fields. Doctors, lawyers, engineers, architects, journalists, freelance writers, educators, and people in most other professions are prime newsletter candidates. Since most professions already have their own professional journals, newsletters must center on one particular aspect of the field. That's why you'll find successful newsletters devoted exclusively to such topics as the copyright law, tax angles for doctors, and getting school budgets passed. Each handles its own particular subject in much greater depth than could a catch-all professional journal which must carry articles on all aspects of the profession.

Program Booklets: When non-profit organizations sponsor fund-raising events such as dinner-dances, variety shows, and even door-to-door solicitations, they often issue souvenir or program booklets to be handed out to those who attend the event or contribute to the drive. Local businesses are asked to insert advertisements in these booklets to pay for their publication and provide revenue for the organization. You can coordinate the preparation and printing of these booklets on behalf of such organizations. You direct the volunteers in soliciting ads, guide the layout of the individual pages, and arrange for the printing. Although this can be done on a straight fee basis, the usual arrangement is for you to receive a percentage of the advertising revenues. Fifteen percent is typical.

Real Estate Directory: Classified ad publications devoted exclusively to real estate listings have been unusually successful in many parts of the United States. Although general circulation newspapers contain real estate classified columns, these are generally limited in scope. Hence the popularity of real estate directories that contain hundreds of listings. The revenues come from (1) advertisements placed by the various brokers, and (2) the price paid by buyers who pick up copies of the directory on the newsstand. Such publications are usually issued once or twice a month.

Recreational Vehicle Directory: The popularity of campers, travel trailers, and motor homes has created the need in many areas for classified ad publications in which people can list, or search for, used RVs that have been placed on the market. RV directories are distributed in the same manner as boat directories, described earlier.

Regional Guide: Tourists visiting your area want to know what there is to do and see, and you can capitalize on this desire by publishing a guide to local attractions. Your revenue comes mainly from advertising inserted by businesses who cater to visitors: restaurants, sightseeing attractions, parks, theaters, etc. Usually the guides are distributed free to hotels and motels, where they are placed in lobby racks and on nightstands in each room.

Regional Magazine: Regional magazines are like any other magazine, except that the bulk of their articles and features play up places and people of interest in the region, and their advertising comes largely from regional business firms. In addition to informative articles, they usually also contain listings of coming events. They are sold on newsstands and through subscriptions.

Road Maps: Anyone can buy an atlas of U.S. roads for four or five dollars, but when it comes to finding local roads, streets, and highways, the national atlas generally cannot do the job. That's why local street maps, sold on newsstands for a dollar or two, are genuine money-makers. And you don't have to be a cartographer to get into this business. It can be as simple as obtaining a city, town, or county road map compiled by the local planning department and having it reproduced. You gain extra revenue by selling advertising space along the borders.

Self-Study Course: The quest for knowledge never ends, and many people prefer to do their studying at home during hours of their own choosing. That's why self-study courses are so popular. Provided you have knowledge that other people are willing to pay for, you can get into this business quite inexpensively because of the availability of low-cost photo offset printing. Many home study courses selling for $50 or more contain no more material than can be found in a $10 book. The way the material is presented makes the difference. The usual format is to present a page or two of new information and follow this up with a question-and-answer review, and then follow each lesson (the equivalent of a chapter in a book) with a review and quiz. It's often called "programmed learning" and it works quite well—both for the course's students and for its vendor.

Shopping Paper: "Shoppers," as they are usually called, consist almost entirely of advertising. They are distributed free, either through the mail or by hand, and they compete successfully with regular newspapers for the advertiser's dollar. I know of one shopper that got started as little more than a four-page handbill. The publisher's starting budget was not large enough to cover typesetting, so she hand-lettered each of the ads before pasting them up onto layout sheets and taking them to the offset printer. Later, she purchased special typewriters that enabled her to set type in professional-looking fonts.

Special Interest Magazine: You read earlier of controlled circulation magazines, each published to serve a particular business field. Their counterpart in the consumer market is the special interest magazine catering to hobby and other personal interests. These, however, are not distributed free. Because they are specialized—perhaps too specialized to appeal to the general public—you won't find them on many newsstands. They are sold mainly through subscriptions. A special interest magazine with a circulation of as little as 35,000 can do quite well financially. Advertisers who make or sell products geared to the special interest of the magazine know that they'll be reaching the very people who are interested in their products.

Street Directory: Street directories are similar to phone books, except that the listings are arranged differently. Each listing contains the street and number followed by the names of the residents at each address, their phone numbers and, sometimes, their occupations. Some directories go so far as to have three separate sections. Following the first listing, as described above, there is an alphabetical listing based on residents' names; and the third section is based on phone numbers, which are listed in numerical order along with the associated names and addresses. The information is obtained from the regular phone book and can be supplemented by sending out inquiry cards to addresses for which there is no phone book listing.

Syndicated Column: You can be a columnist if you can provide information that many newspaper readers would like to know. You can get started by syndicating your own column and then, when enough newspapers have signed up to prove its value, you can offer it to an established syndicate and have them handle the business details for you from there on out. Or you can continue to syndicate your own material and skip having to share the income with a syndicate. How do you get started? Do what Michael V. did, as explained later in this chapter.

Syndicated Editorials: If you've ever read editorials in the local paper—or heard them on local radio stations—you may have detected that the writers have difficulty coming up with good material time after time. You can be a big help by writing editorials and then syndicating them to smaller newspapers and radio stations. The standard fee is a dollar per editorial, with the customer receiving five or six per week. Thus you get a minimum of $260 a year from each client. Two hundred clients (and that's not too much to expect when you consider that there are thousands of small radio stations and newspapers) can bring you an income of $52,000 a year.

Tablemat News: The morning's news on a restaurant tablemat; it's a unique business idea that has proven successful. Review Chapter 4 for details.

Topical Jokes: Earlier we spoke of selling patter to disc jockeys. In a similar vein you can sell topical jokes to public speakers of all kinds. Who are the candidates for such a publication? Top business executives, politicians, comedy writers—and anyone who can benefit from being able to come up with one- and two-liners keyed to current events. You need a vivid sense of imagination in order to find the humorous angle to items in the news, but if you have this, there's room for you to join the several existing topical humor publications. That's because everybody sees things in a different light, and your original material will not be the same as anybody else's. I know one man who is called on to give several speeches each month and subscribes to four such services.

Trade Directory: There is an excellent market for national directories listing all the businesses in a given field. Among the buyers of such directories are other business firms that sell to members of the industry covered by a particular directory. You can find out if a directory already exists for any field by checking *Subject Guide to Books in Print* and the *Directory of National Trade Associations* at your local library.

Vanity Publishing: Let others do the writing for you and pay you for it as well. You can be a subsidy or "vanity" publisher— one who converts manuscripts into books for budding writers. After they have grown tired of rejection slips from regular publishers, some writers are more than willing to underwrite the cost of publishing their material in book form. Do you have to own a printing press to be a book publisher? Decidedly not. The majority of all publishers in the United States send their work to outside printers. The difference between what you pay the printer and what the author pays you can be more than a thousand dollars per book. Why are you needed? Because you will have searched out printers who can do the most professional job at the most reasonable rates. And you will have helped the author to improve the style and content of his or her manuscript. The finished product should be considerably better than if the author had tried to do everything alone.

HOW TO START AND RUN YOUR PUBLISHING BUSINESS

Even though there are 38 different publishing fields listed in this chapter, there are some general rules that apply regardless of which field you enter. Following these rules will help you to get started easier and make money faster. Here they are:

1. Buy as little equipment as possible, farming out as much of the work as you can.
2. Use other people's money as capital for your project.
3. Start small, gain experience, and grow as you learn.

Now let's examine each of these rules individually and see how they have helped others to get started in low-investment, high-profit publishing enterprises.

RULE #1:
Buy as Little Equipment as Possible

The mainstay of the publishing business is, of course, the printing press, but it doesn't have to be *your* printing press. Nor do you need a lot of other equipment that might, at first glance, seem necessary in a publishing business. Even if your initial investment were not under $1,500, I'd say the same thing. The money is far better spent in developing your product and your customer list. When possible, especially at the outset, buy a service instead of a machine. Let others do as much of the physical work for you as possible.

Ernest F. followed this rule in launching his book publishing business. He started with a 50-page how-to booklet showing home craftsmen how they could make money with woodworking tools.

"My goal was to develop a complete line of several dozen booklets on various ways to make money at home in one's spare time," Ernie explains, "and at first I thought it would be economical to do the printing myself. But when I examined my budget and the amount of time I had available, I soon realized that neither my limited dollars nor my limited hours would be sufficient. So after writing that first booklet, I took it to a local printer, and I've been doing the same ever since."

Ernie advertised his booklet through a classified ad in *Popular Science*. The first ad brought 72 orders for the booklet that sold for $5.95. Even though the pamphlet had few pages, it contained a lot of helpful information, and readers were well satisfied with it. Expanding his advertising campaign with the profits received from the initial sales, Ernie sold thousands of copies and then set out to publish booklets in various other home money-making fields.

"I now have the several dozen titles I had originally envisioned," Ernie reports, "and a few of those volumes are full-sized, hard-cover books. And, oh yes, we do have a printing press now. But it's not used to print the books. We use it to print our catalogs and sales letters."

Ernie started his business with $1,250. The part-time venture has become full-time and it's netting him an average of a thousand dollars a week.

RULE #2:
Use Other People's Money

Using other people's money to develop your business is one of the keys to success in any enterprise. Usually, one goes to a bank or other lender, but in many of the publishing businesses listed in this chapter, you don't need to do that. You can make legal use of other people's money without signing any notes and without having to pay any interest.

Consider what Gayle T. did with her business based on looseleaf guides with updates. Gayle had long been a real estate salesperson in her home town, and a very successful one. So successful, in fact, that she felt she could make even more money by sharing her sales techniques with other real estate salespeople across the country. She could, in effect, sell what she knew about selling real estate.

"I typed out a 272-page guide to successful real estate selling," Gayle reports. "But real estate is a volatile profession. There are always new developments, new laws, new opportunities, and new challenges that change the nature of the business. I soon realized that my guide would be quickly outdated . . . unless it were updated."

Gayle's decision was not to sell the guide alone, but to sell it with a continuing subscription of monthly updates, each consisting of a four-page insert that the customer could read and then place in the proper spot in the looseleaf binder.

"I offered the guide and update for $10 a month, billable monthly, or for $89, cash-in-advance. Enough people took advantage of the cash-in-advance savings to foot the printing bill. The guide was published within six weeks."

What if not enough people had ordered it? "Then I would have refunded their money and I would have been out the amount I spent on advertising. But that's far better than if I had printed the book first, only to discover it wouldn't sell. This way, all I was gambling with was the advertising cash and my time in writing the guide."

Gayle now has a thousand subscribers. Half of the $100,000 in proceeds is clear profit.

I sense that you have a question: Is it ethical to offer a product before you actually have it on hand, ready to deliver? All I can say is that it is common practice. Even the nation's largest companies test-advertise new products before they are actually produced. If, however, you are not able to deliver a product ordered through the mail within 30 days, you must notify the customer and make an offer to refund his money.

"I did that," Gayle notes, "because the finished guide was not actually ready from the printer for about 40 days after my first orders were received. Ninety percent of those who had ordered elected to wait for delivery. And of the ten percent who asked for their money back, nearly half bought the guide later when I informed them that it was ready."

RULE #3:
Start Small and Grow as You Learn

It's better to be a wader before you become a swimmer, especially in the publishing field. By getting your feet wet before you tackle the big waves, you learn more about what the water is like—and you can deal with it more effectively.

Michael V. had an idea for a syndicated column on history. "It would contain little-known anecdotes about our American heritage," he explains. "I started thinking about it early in our Bicentennial Year. I wrote up some sample columns and sent them off to a number of the country's largest newspaper syndicates, only to get rejection slips from every last one of them."

But Michael was convinced that his idea was a good one and that the column could remain interesting and highly readable even long after the Bicentennial Year had passed. Undaunted by the rejection slips, he decided to syndicate it on his own. But not immediately.

"What I did first," he reports, "was to offer it free to the publisher of my local newspaper. He liked it fine (how could he argue with the price?) and this helped me in two ways. First, I gained experience in writing the column and I learned through the reader mail how it could be improved. And second, I was able to use reproductions of that original column to show other editors what it looked like. Each week I went to the library and looked up the names of 20 or 30 editors in various parts of the country. I sent them tear sheets of the column and before long I had signed up 60 papers, each paying me $5 for the weekly column."

Michael had, in effect, started his own syndicate. And one day it dawned on him that he could sell other material to newspapers as well.

"I didn't have the time or knowledge to prepare more columns on my own," he recalls, "so I sent a notice to a writers' magazine asking for free-lancers to send me ideas for columns they'd like to write."

The response was more than Michael expected, and from the many ideas received he chose two to offer to his customers and, in fact, to hundreds of other papers across the country. He rented a mailing list to save time in copying the names and addressing the envelopes, and he signed up enough papers to make the new columns profitable.

His syndicate has continued to grow, and now it also includes tape recordings that are distributed to radio stations. The firm is currently syndicating a dozen features to the print and broadcast media. Michael has received several offers from large syndicates seeking to buy him out, and he has rejected them all.

BE A PUBLISHING "MAGNET"

You've probably heard the expression "publishing magnate." My dictionary describes a magnate as a powerful or influential person. Although that's what you might become if you enter the publishing field, I suggest that "magnet" is a more appropriate word. Pick the right plan from this chapter and you could well be a publishing magnet—attracting more money than you've ever seen before.

10

Top-Paying Camera and Art Projects

If you're into photography or art as a hobby, and you have a flair for it, excellent money awaits you as the operator of a spare-time business based on the skills and knowledge you have acquired. Your photographic or artistic equipment can be tools providing you with a lot more income than you thought possible.

Up until now you may have thought of your photographic or artistic abilities merely as a means of expressing yourself, but in this chapter we'll be talking about many different ways to convert those skills into practical money-making projects. And you don't have to be an artistic genius to succeed—all you have to be is technically competent. In other words, this chapter shows how you can convert ordinary skills into an extraordinary income.

HOW TO MAKE BIG MONEY IN PHOTOGRAPHY OR ART

It's just as easy—perhaps even easier—to perform profitable work with a camera or artist's brush as it is to do work that is merely for one's own pleasure. The key to making big money in photography or art is this:

Don't sell a picture—sell a service.

Find a way that your camera, darkroom equipment, or drawing board can serve others, and you have found a way to make a lot of money. There are 39 such ways described in this chapter. Let's look at just one example.

HOW $1,000 BRINGS IN THAT MUCH PER WEEK

Calvin P. has built a thriving spare-time business by going to dress rehearsals, camera in hand. Cal's specialty is taking cast photographs of amateur theatricals and variety shows. He snaps pictures of what is happening on stage and then returns on a night when the regular performance is given to let the cast members see the various shots he has taken and place orders for their own copies.

"Performing in an amateur show is an important event in the lives of nearly all the participants," Cal explains, "and they find it hard to resist buying one or more of my 'action' shots as mementos. On the average, I find that about two thirds of the cast members of a particular show will buy at least one picture."

Cal closely follows the papers in a three-county area, looking for announcements of forthcoming amateur shows. Then he contacts someone who is in authority in the sponsoring organization and explains his service.

"I point out that 10% of my proceeds will be turned over to the club treasury, and they find the idea hard to resist," he reports. "There are two reasons why I take the pictures at dress rehearsals rather than at actual performances," he notes. "First, if I have to use a strobe light instead of the existing stage lighting, it would be annoying during a regular performance. And second, having the samples ready to show after a regular performance gives me an opportunity to speak with all the cast members—and to do so while they still feel the excitement of the performance. They are definitely in a buying mood."

Cal offers 5 x 7 inch photos inserted in an attractive cardboard frame for $4.75 each. Such a variety of shots is offered that most customers buy at least two.

"Naturally, each person buys the shots in which he or she appears, and if a person happens to be in several shots, then there's the potential of selling several shots to that person. When they want more than one copy of a single shot, the price drops to $3.75."

Because his territory includes all of three counties, Cal is able to "cover" an average of seven amateur shows each week. Gross sales per show average out at $200. Here's the financial breakdown:

```
Gross sales ............. $1400.00
10% donation  ..........   140.00
Net proceeds ...........   1260.00
Expenses (20%) ........    252.00
Net profit ............. $1008.00
```

Although he attends seven dress rehearsals each week, Cal has found that most of them are on Tuesday, Wednesday, or Thursday nights. Thus some nights find him at two or three different locations. And since most actual performances are on Friday or Saturday nights, he's busy those two evenings as well.

"It's become a full-time business with me," Cal says. "When I started, I was hitting about half as many shows and earning about half as much money. It soon became clear that doubling my effort would double my profit. So I gave up my job as a school teacher, knowing that I'd never be able to earn the $50,000 there that I am earning here. And even though my evenings are kept quite full, the days are mostly my own—except for an hour or two spent in the darkroom." Thus for about 30 hours of work per week, using camera and darkroom equipment that cost him $1,000, Cal is earning that much each week.

39 CAMERA AND EASEL PROJECTS TO CHOOSE FROM

There are hundreds of ways you can make an excellent part- or full-time living in a camera or art-based business. Most of them are variations of the 39 basic methods in this listing.

Aerial Photography: Charter a light plane with pilot for $40-$50 and you should be able to come up with enough saleable shots to earn five times as much. Take pictures of business establishments, clusters of homes, shopping malls, downtown business districts, and recreational facilities. Then show samples to the owners or operators of the establishments you've photographed. It's hard for a business owner, municipal agency, chamber of commerce, or even private home owner to turn down such a photo. I know a police officer who moonlights in this way—making several photo-flights every month—and earns as much in his spare-time endeavor as he does on the force.

Art Consultant: No creative ability is needed for this business—merely a recognition of what is pleasing and attractive and an acquaintance with a number of local artists. You find original art that can grace the walls of business and professional offices, hotel, motel, and apartment house lobbies, restaurants, cocktail lounges, and even private homes. You earn double money by collecting a fee from your clients and a commission from the artists whose work you sell. You can build up a list of clients by becoming known as a local authority, and you can do this in one or more of several ways: write a local newspaper column on art, speak before civic and social groups, or teach an adult education course on art appreciation. Free publicity is the key.

Art Instruction: If you have a way with oils, have obtained a degree of local recognition, and can get along easily with other people, then you can start your own art school. Teach students individually at your home or theirs, or for a higher hourly fee, teach groups. You can usually rent a church or civic hall for a nominal amount. Then, as the number of your students and classes increases, you can add other teachers to your staff.

Breed Show Photography: This is similar to the type of photography that Calvin P. does, except that instead of going to amateur theatricals you are going to dog shows, and instead of photographing people you are photographing prize-winning canines. What owner of a "best-in-breed" could refuse such shots? By donating a small percentage of your proceeds to the sponsoring club, you can get advance designation as the official show photographer.

Business Logos: Logo is short for logotype. It's similar to a trademark, and many business firms like to have distinctive logos to display in their advertising and on their letterheads. The drawings are usually simple but dramatic, and their purpose is to provide a symbol that people instantly associate with the company it represents. So if you can draw well, and can come up with unique ideas, you can make good money creating logos for all kinds of local businesses.

Calligraphy: With an italic fountain pen (or, sometimes, an artist's brush) you can cash in on the demand for artistic handwriting known as calligraphy. It is used on scrolls presented to people who are being honored at a special occasion, on invitations to such events as weddings and bar mitzvahs, and on plaques that customers present as gifts to their friends and relatives. You can learn various lettering styles from books in the library. A good one is *Learning Calligraphy* by Margaret Shepherd, published by

Macmillan. And you can solicit customers by running small classified ads in the paper. As your business grows, however, most of your business will come through word-of-mouth. People who possess your work will be showing it off and identifying you as its creator.

Caricatures: Hundreds of people across the United States have developed top-paying spare- and full-time businesses by setting themselves up with an easel at shopping malls, flea markets, bazaars, and country fairs. They draw quick caricatures of interested passersby, charging about $7.50 each. Each caricature (a comically exaggerated likeness of the customer) takes about ten minutes to produce. Giving yourself a breathing spell in between customers, you should be able to average four caricatures an hour. That means you can take in better than $240 for each eight-hour period.

Custom Framing: Pieces of art come in so many assorted sizes that it's often difficult to find attractive frames to match them. And that's where the custom framer comes in. You can do the work in a basement shop with materials available at any art supply store. You obtain assignments by running classified ads, dropping off business cards at art shows, and installing posters or cards on the community bulletin boards that are located in supermarkets and variety stores.

Custom Processing: Most of us send our film to a commercial processing firm that runs it through a machine quickly and inexpensively. That's fine for the everyday camera bug, but the serious photographer often requires special handling of his work. You can provide custom developing and enlarging, meeting the customer's specifications concerning exposure times, cropping, special papers, and vignetting. A listing in the Yellow Pages and perhaps a small ad in some of the photography magazines should bring you plenty of work.

Custom T-Shirts: T-shirts featuring custom lettering or decals are in demand by bowling teams, schools, summer camps, and a variety of private organizations. The decal transfer machines used to do this work can be bought for a few hundred dollars.

Darkroom Rental: A lot of amateur photographers would like occasional access to a darkroom to work on their films and enlargements. Their need is not large enough to warrant going out and buying equipment of their own, so these people are willing to pay for the use of someone else's. By having several enlargers and a variety of trays, reels, and tanks, you can meet their needs. In addition to charging for darkroom time you'll earn money from the sale of papers and chemicals used by each customer.

Decoupage: Many people have become adept at decoupage (the art of attaching paper cutouts to wood and then covering it with layers of varnish or lacquer), but money-making opportunities still exist. One person I know has gone into the decoupage menu business. She sells restaurants on the idea of having their menus decoupaged. It's unique when compared with dog-eared and stained paper menus, and it's a repeat business (every time the prices go up, she gets a new batch of orders). Another person has an arrangement with a local calligrapher. They send work to each other. Whenever the calligrapher gets an assignment for a piece of work that he feels should be decoupaged, he sends it to her. And when customers come to her seeking some decoupage that needs elegant hand-lettering, she works in tandem with her calligrapher friend.

Executive Portraits: Whether you work in film or in oil, using the term "executive portraits" can bring you many added assignments, and higher prices as well. A photographer in a Midwestern city who started out by advertising that he did portrait work didn't reach his peak until he ran an ad stating that he did executive portraits. Since most people are status-seekers, going to a photographer who specializes in executive portraits fills an ego need. Many of his clients are, indeed, executives. But then many are not in that category at all; they merely hope that his portraits will make them look like executives, and he earns top money fulfilling those desires.

Greeting Card Sketches: We live in an impersonal age, and that's why good money can usually be made by adding a personal touch. Greeting cards are an example. One way to do this is to have people provide you with a photograph of their home. From this, you do a line drawing that can be used on holiday greeting cards and stationery. It can be a local business or a mail order operation.

Insurance Pictures: People who own sailboats, cabin cruisers, motor homes, and private airplanes sometimes have difficulty after accidents or fires convincing insurance companies of the extent of their losses. You can provide a valuable service by taking a series of photos of these possessions, along with all of the accessories that have been installed. One company goes so far as to take TV tape recordings of the exteriors and interiors of boats. Then, should a loss ever occur, the boat owner has 30 minutes of tape as proof of how the boat was equipped.

Kids Action Photos: Most parents take snapshots of their kids, but rarely do the pictures do justice to the youngsters. The pictures either appear stilted or, if they show action, are poorly framed and focused. Specialize in the type of photography that shows kids at play and do it well, and you'll have a waiting list of customers.

Mall Portraits: With a portrait camera and a suitable backdrop, you can do a thriving business at shopping malls by serving impulse customers. What's an "impulse" customer? That's a person who had no intention of buying a portrait until he or she passed your booth, saw you at work, and saw some of your earlier portraits on display. Most mall portrait businesses stay in one location for only a week or so and then move on to another mall. Rental fees for lobby space are moderate.

Model Home or Apartment Renderings: Even the best photographer usually cannot depict a model home or apartment as enticingly as can the artist who does a sketch of the same subject. That's why builders often turn to free-lance artists to illustrate their sales and rental brochures. Draw up a few samples and send them out to likely prospects in the building business and you should find yourself with plenty of work.

Painting Restoration: If you have, or can acquire, a knack for cleaning up and restoring old oil paintings, there's plenty of business waiting for you. It can be a mail order operation, drawing customers from all over the country, or you can obtain local assignments from antique dealers, art shops, and private owners.

Pastel Portraits: These sell for between four and ten dollars and they sell particularly well at locations where people are out to have a good time, such as bazaars, recreation areas, theme parks, flea markets, resorts, and historical areas. Get permission to set up your easel and a display rack, and then proceed to do quick pastel likenesses of passersby who spot your work and would like a portrait of their own.

Pet Portraits: No, the pet doesn't come to your studio and sit for its portrait. Instead, its owner sends you a photo of Fido or Tabby or Flicka, and you send back the photo accompanied by a drawing you have copied from the photo. One of the best ways to advertise is to run small magazine ads with side-by-side reproductions of a pet photo and the drawing that resulted from it.

Photo Features: Hundreds of specialty magazines are searching for new material to include in their monthly issues, and the easiest thing to sell them is photo features. These are brief articles accompanied by a series of photos that almost tell the stories by themselves. Pick a subject that interests you (historical places, crafts projects, home improvements, hobby collections) and start shooting. You'll make more sales if you specialize in one topic and become known as a photo journalist in that field. Writers' books in the local library will tell you how to go about this.

Photo Paintings: This is another way that artists can make money in mail order. It works in much the same manner as pet portraits, listed previously, but under this plan people send you photos of prized possessions instead of pets. They get in return an oil painting of their home, boat, place of business, etc.

Posters: Hand-lettered or silk-screened posters have not been entirely replaced by commercial printing. For several reasons, businessmen and community groups still require the hand-done variety. This happens when (1) the number of copies required does not warrant the expense of mechanical printing, and (2) the need is for lavish colors or unusual designs that would be impractical to reproduce mechanically. You can save money for others and make money for yourself by starting a poster service.

Prints Galore: Many people who do not want to spend the money for oil paintings to grace their homes or business establishments nevertheless appreciate art and are prime prospects for art reproductions. You can open a print shop in your home, as a mall booth, or even on a temporary basis at flea markets. The initial investment for prints can be as little as $500. Check the small ads in the back pages of women's and art magazines for print manufacturers and distributors; also pore through the wholesale gift catalogs. One budding print dealer of my acquaintance went to a department store and wrote down the names of the manufacturers that were printed in small type at the bottom and on the reverse of prints she found on display there.

Publicity Shots: They say that a picture is worth a thousand words, and when it comes to publicity in the newspaper, this can be especially true. Editors don't like publicity shots that show a bunch of people lined up side by side, but they will often print shots showing people in action. Keep this in mind as you accept assignments doing publicity shots for business firms and charitable organizations. After a number of your pictures have been printed in the papers, put together a portfolio to show other prospective clients.

Real Estate Photography: Real estate brokers spend a lot of time showing homes to prospective buyers who sometimes reject a home on first sight. That's why smart brokers like to show photos of their listed homes before taking a client to the place. Trouble is, many real estate people don't know how to take photos that do justice to their property offerings. Work out a contract deal with such brokers to handle all of their photographic work and you'll develop a continuing income.

Resort Photography: People on vacation at resort areas are generally in a relaxed and happy mood. Many of them have made new friends, and group photos of them and their friends having fun are highly saleable items. If you live in an area where bus tours frequently stop, you can arrange with the tour operator to have the people line up for a group shot; this may be the only opportunity they have to get a photo of the entire group. No tour groups? Then you may have to be a bit more enterprising. In an old New England town, there's a man who earns his keep throughout the summer months by having an old buggy parked on a downtown street and inviting passersby to climb aboard and pose for a photo, which they can pick up from him at the same spot the next day. In this kind of business, you are limited only by your imagination.

Roving Art Gallery: One of the most difficult things about running an art gallery is getting people to stop by. It can take a lot of advertising and word-of-mouth to get firmly established. This problem can be largely avoided if you go to the people instead of hoping that they'll come to you. There are many ways to do this. The most obvious, of course, is arranging to place art on display at shopping malls and flea markets. Other possibilities include selling out of a motor home parked outside shopping centers, arranging for art "shows" in movie theater lobbies and in banks, and having civic-minded people sponsor art "showings" in their homes as fund-raising projects. Their favorite charity gets 10% of the proceeds, you keep 15%, and the rest goes to the artists who created the works that are sold.

Sculpture Reproductions: There's a tremendous market for reproductions of famous statues, and once you form a "master" in clay and use it to create a mold, you can use that mold to produce profitable reproductions that will sell for years to come. Your output can be sold to gift shops, mail order specialty houses, department stores, and through the mail. One artistic entrepreneur built up an inventory of 20 different pieces and then formed a mini-statue-of-the-month club, offering members a different reproduction each month.

Sensitized Photos: Many photo supply stores sell a chemical preparation known as a photo sensitizer that allows you to reproduce a photograph on just about any object, from beer mugs to T-shirts. The market for such photographic novelties is obvious. You can either sell standard items (such as souvenir photos of a local landmark reproduced on a plate, or made-to-order items such as the customer's picture on a beer stein). Standard items can be distributed to gift shops and mail order houses, while orders for custom-made work can be handled by those same outlets or through your own mail order business. If you can't find sensitizing materials locally, they're available from Rockland Colloid Corp., 599 River Rd., Piermont, NY 10968.

Show Shots: You've already read about this lucrative business, as related in the experience of Calvin P. earlier in this chapter.

Sign Painting: Plastic may seem to have taken over the world, but there's still a need for hand-painted wooden signs. Not every merchant wants the plastic variety, and the demand for sign painters is as great as ever. If you've got a steady hand, a comfortable garage or basement to work in, and a little carpentry ability to go along with your lettering talents, you can set yourself up in the sign-painting business. Don't overlook truck-lettering as a source of added revenue.

Silhouettes: This is an art form that was fashionable earlier in this country's history—and it's back now. Set yourself up in a booth at a mall, a crafts show, in a tourist spot, or at a flea market, display some of your work, and customers will soon be sitting for quick silhouette portraits. An advantage of this business is that you don't need to be an artist at all. By placing your customer between a spotlight and a small screen, you can trace the silhouette that is projected on the screen. Then copy the tracing onto a piece of black construction paper, cut out along the lines and, pronto, you have an attractive silhouette portrait.

Talking Heads: Here's a great promotion item that goes over big in stores and at trade shows. Many people won't pay any particular attention to a film or slide presentation that is set up on a countertop—but what do you think they do if they spot a mannequin that is talking? They stop and take notice! Getting a mannequin to talk is simpler than it seems. You use a Super-8 sound camera and make a movie of a person giving the sales presentation. The filming should involve a close-up of the person's head. Then you project that close-up onto the mannequin's head. It appears as if the dummy is actually speaking. Such displays were hits on the Freedom Train and at the Smithsonian Institution, and now entrepreneurs are introducing them in stores and at trade shows as well.

Tintypes: Just as silhouettes were popular in this country's past and have now been revived, the same is true of tintypes. One way to simulate the tintypes of the 1880's is the sensitized photo process mentioned earlier. Locating an old tintype camera can be difficult and expensive, so some practitioners use a modern camera hidden inside a wooden box that looks like an old camera. Then they go to crafts shows, historic sites, and shopping centers to perform their services.

Visual Aids: You can be of considerable assistance to people who give training lectures at seminars, symposiums, and conventions. Plain lecturing is old hat; multi-media presentations are in, so most lecturers like to have their talks illustrated with slides, charts, movies, or TV tapes. Pick a specialty along one or more of these lines and then contact company training directors, seminar sponsors, lecture bureaus, and educational institutions.

Wedding Photos: The arrival of the easy-to-make snapshot put many portrait studios out of business, but there's still plenty of work for wedding photographers. The families of the bride and groom are too involved in the Big Event to take pictures themselves—and besides, they want to be assured of high quality remembrances. So they hire a wedding photographer—who might as well be you.

Yacht Renderings: Some people invest almost as much money in their pleasure craft as they do in their homes (sometimes more) and they are understandably proud of these expensive possessions. That's why they are prime prospects for oil paintings or drawings of their boats, to be hung in their dens and admired during the winter months when they can't be sailing. You can solicit yacht-owner customers by advertising in the boating sections of local newspapers, or you can run a mail order operation by advertising in the boating magazines and having the yachtsmen send color photos of their craft.

HOW TO PICK YOUR OWN GRAPHIC ARTS SPECIALTY

As you've seen in the list of camera and art projects, there are two elements in building a successful business:

1. Creating a product that is attractive and desirable.
2. Finding the best way to sell that product in sufficient volume to pay you well for your efforts.

Please note that the word "product" has been used in each of the elements. It's important to remember that while you may be producing and selling art, you must treat it as merchandise. This may be difficult if you've always thought of yourself as producing art for art's sake. In the terms of this book, however, you are producing art not only for personal satisfaction, but also for personal financial gain—as much gain as you can get.

That's why, as you study and re-study the list of projects, you should follow this rule:

Base your selection not only on your ability to produce the type of item listed but also on the available methods of selling that product.

A WINNING COMBINATION

The project listings contained in this chapter are from a file that I frequently show to friends and clients who are interested in starting a camera or art-based business. One such person who sought my advice was Linda T. When she saw the section on caricatures, an immediate smile crossed Linda's face. It was followed by a frown.

"Why, I've been doing caricatures for years," was her first reaction. "I'd love to be able to make money at it."

Then she read further and saw that, as listed, the project requires traveling to do the work "on location" at such places as malls and fairs.

"I can't travel," Linda explained. "I have three young children, one of them not even in school yet. This would be out of the question."

I had a surprise for her. "Read the section on greeting card sketches," I suggested.

She did so and then commented, "I'm not very good at drawing buildings. I've always concentrated on people."

"I'm not talking about the subject matter," I explained. "Remember, we're discussing a way for you to make money. Look at how the greeting card sketches are sold."

"You mean," she asked, "that I could sell caricatures through the mail?"

"Yes, by having people send you a photograph of the person to be 'caricatured' and basing your drawing on that photo."

Linda gave it serious thought—not only during that conference with me, but also in the weeks ahead. Before long she had set herself up in the mail order caricature business. She's done exceedingly well, getting customers from ads she runs in a number of magazines. The work is done from the comfort of her home, and she's able to fit it in easily around her busy homemaker's schedule.

The point, then, is that you should study the project listing in this chapter at least twice:

1. Read them to find the types of photographic or artistic products you are able to produce.
2. Then read through all the projects again to see which sales methods from other types of projects can be adapted to the kind of work you'd like to do.

In most of the project listings, I've included several possible sales methods. You need not, however, be confined to these methods. By borrowing and adapting from the other projects in the listing you can come up with a winning combination that best fits your own circumstances—a money-making project that can easily meet or even surpass your financial goals.

A STEP-BY-STEP GUIDE TO STARTING
AND RUNNING YOUR CAMERA OR ART BUSINESS

Regardless of which camera or art-based product you choose and no matter what selling method you decide upon, there are four steps you should follow to build your project to maximum profit levels:

1. Maximize your volume and efficiency
2. Make your product as "self-selling" as possible

3. Diversify with other products

4. Expand your production with the work of others

We'll examine each of these steps individually, illustrating each one with examples of how it has been carried out in one of the projects presented in this chapter.

STEP ONE:
Maximize Your Volume and Efficiency

Up until now your camera or art-based hobby probably has been treated as just that, a hobby. You've taken your time, perhaps experimented with new techniques, and then sat back to admire your work. But from now on, your goal will be maximum efficiency and **production**. And you can easily achieve it because you will be concentrating on one basic product.

Let's say you're a camera bug. You've taken pictures of your vacation trips, your family members, and perhaps have dabbled in portraiture or scenic shots. Each picture you have taken has been different from the previous one, and so each has taken you extra time to produce. But when you set yourself up in one of the camera projects listed in this chapter, you will not be doing this.

It's time to let you in on an important secret behind the success of a camera-based project:

Instead of taking many different pictures under many different circumstances, you will be taking what is basically the same picture over and over again.

Howard C. specializes in real estate photography. In his spare-time business he takes 35-mm slides of homes that his client-brokers have listed for sale. He provides each of the brokers with a desktop machine that automatically displays a carousel of slides. This makes it convenient for the broker to show potential buyers what is available; when a particular home appeals to them, they are taken to see it.

"This saves the broker a lot of wasted time taking people out to places they would not be interested in," Howard explains.

While it's not quite true that every photograph of a home is shot in exactly the same manner, Howard has honed it down nearly to a science.

"Once I arrive at the site, the entire process takes less than five minutes," he reports. "First I drive past the home and look for the best angle to shoot from. Once that's determined, I park the car as close to that spot as I can, get out, and shoot three or four pictures. Then I'm off to the next location. It's not unusual for me to take 50 or 75 home pictures on a weekend day."

Howard's business serves more than two dozen brokers in his and several neighboring communities. Thanks to his cost-effective techniques, he earns an average of $125 for each weekend day he works.

Let's look at some of the other photographic projects listed in this chapter and see how efficiency techniques can be employed:

- *Aerial Photography.* Many shots of many different subjects are taken during each flight. And later in the darkroom many of the shots can be cut up into smaller photos. An aerial photographer can often take a picture of a cluster of buildings and then produce individual blowups of each structure, selling each blowup to the owner of the particular building.

- *Breed Show Photography.* The way to maximize efficiency here is to catch the prize-winning owners and their animals immediately after the prizes have been awarded. Trying to round them up later can waste a lot of time and cause you to miss important shots.

- *Custom Processing.* The basis of your business is to do work that is customized for the individual client, but this doesn't mean you have to spend hours doing it. One custom processor I know uses a modified assembly-line technique; he "bunches" his work so that everything of a similar nature is done together. Then he moves on to the next type of project. Thus he doesn't have to be constantly changing his chemicals, papers, or enlarger easels. "I've been able to double my output this way," he reports.

- *Sensitized Photos.* In personalizing beer steins with the customer's photographic likeness, Ron A. uses many of the mass production techniques referred to in Chapter 2. "I depend on volume to make my money," Ron states, "and I accomplish that by piling up 50 or so orders and then processing them on a step-by-step basis, performing the same step on the entire lot before moving on to the next procedure."

Can efficiency techniques be used on art-based projects as well as on photographic work? You bet. In her caricature work, for example, Linda T. uses a set of five standard backgrounds. These are simple but funny scenes serving as a backdrop for the caricature. To increase her output, Linda draws many of the backgrounds in advance, particularly during slow periods. "This allows me to 'average out' my workload," she explains, "so that when new orders come in I can process them much more rapidly than would otherwise be possible."

STEP TWO:
Make Your Product as "Self-Selling" as Possible

Everything else being equal, the more time you can devote to producing products and the less time you must spend selling them, the better off you'll be. If you make your item as "self-selling" as possible you can produce more products—and earn more money.

While nothing totally sells itself, in many cases you can choose a sales method that comes pretty close to it. These are some examples:

- Booths at flea markets, bazaars, and in malls where passersby see you at work, examine your display of previous work, and wait in line for their turn to pose for you.
- Customers who display work they have purchased from you and recommend you to their friends.
- Mail order ads with illustrations showing precisely what the customer will get from you.
- Contract arrangements worked out in advance with real estate brokers, amateur theatrical producers, breed show sponsors, resort owners, yacht clubs, and other groups who can help you sell your work in volume.
- Arrangements made with gift shops, department stores, and mail order houses to buy your work in wholesale lots.

Sandra R. makes excellent money preparing personalized greeting cards for people who respond to her mail order ads. The ads she places in national magazines depict exactly what the customer is going to get. They show, side by side, a photograph of a home and a greeting card cover with a line drawing of that same home.

"I even have a money-back-if-not-completely-satisfied policy," Sandra notes, "but nobody has ever taken me up on it. They've seen from the ad what I'm going to do for them—and they get what the ad says they'll get."

After receiving a photo of the customer's home, Sandra makes the line drawing and takes it to a printer who reproduces it on standard card stock.

"I've gotten so that I can make the average drawing in about 15 minutes," Sandra explains. "After all expenses are paid, I'm able to average more than $20 an hour for what I do."

STEP THREE:
Diversify with Other Products

Once you have a customer, why not sell him more than what he bargained for? Offer similar or related items and you'll make extra sales with very little effort. Here's how some of the people you've already met in this chapter are doing it:

- Calvin P., the man who sells photos to performers in amateur theatricals, carries a supply of paper, plastic, and wooden frames with him when he displays the photos he's taken. Nearly half of those who buy the pictures also buy the high quality frames to go with them.

- Linda T., the young housewife who sells personal caricatures through the mail, includes with each order she ships out a little flyer displaying some printed caricatures of well-known people that she also has available. About 10% of her customers place an order for one or more of these—and because the printing cost is so small, the money received is almost total profit.

- Howard C., who specializes in photographing homes for real estate brokers, makes extra sales to these same brokers by offering black and white reproductions of some of the slides he has taken. These black and white photos are then used in local newspaper advertising.

- Sandra R., the greeting card artist, includes with her shipments a slip offering printed stationery. She turns the work over to her printer and is able to pocket 25% of what the customer has paid.

You'll find that in most cases offering additional products will involve very little extra work and a lot of extra profit. And in following this practice you'll be doing precisely what the nation's drug stores, department stores, and discount houses do: you'll be selling to your customers items they had no intention of buying before they placed their main order with you.

STEP FOUR:
Expand Your Production with the Work of Others

As you develop your production and sales techniques, and as the volume of business grows, you may want to consider hiring others to carry part of the workload for you. In fact, if you want to make really big money, that is what you will have to do. And why not? If you can multiply your earnings without multiplying your own working hours, you should latch on to the opportunity. And the opportunity does exist in almost any camera or art project listed in this chapter.

What it requires is the training of other people to carry out the procedures you have developed. The people you choose must, naturally, have artistic or photographic skills similar to your own. If they do, they can be shown how to follow your procedures. Then you can do one or more of the following:

- If you wholesale your output or sell through the mail, you can increase your volume.
- If you sell at booths, you can establish additional booths at new locations.
- If you do "on location" photography, you can handle two or more assignments simultaneously.
- If you do custom work, you can accommodate more customers.

Ashley M. is a commercial photographer who specializes in weddings. Soon after he went into business, Ashley encountered a recurring problem.

"I would have to turn down assignments," he recalls, "because they conflicted with a wedding I had already agreed to photograph. So the business was going to my competitors."

Ashley decided that even if he couldn't photograph the additional weddings personally, he could get a percentage of the money that was paid to photograph them by having one or two friends on call to handle the work when assignments conflicted.

"Naturally, I have to pay these people, but it's a good arrangement for everybody. The additional wedding assignments go to my business instead of a competitor, and the person I hire gets good pay for an afternoon's work without having the responsibility of developing and enlarging the pictures afterwards. I handle the darkroom work during the week. Naturally, I don't make as much profit on these additional weddings as if I had covered them myself, but without this arrangement it's money that would be totally lost to me anyway."

Consider these questions:

- Did the Kentucky Colonel stick to one store because he felt he had to prepare his recipes personally?
- Did Howard Hughes stick to one airplane rather than form an airline with craft piloted by other men?
- Did Thomas Edison refuse to allow other people to produce the products he had invented?

The answer to each of these questions is, of course, no. Each of these people—and thousands of other successful businessmen and women—have recognized the fact that the way to make big money with what they have created is to turn much, if not all, of the production over to others. In your own business you should, at least to some extent, do the same thing.

It can pave the way for almost limitless growth.

11

Earn Big Returns from Small Investments

Investments are not only for the rich. They are also for the future rich. Many people with only a small amount of capital to work with bypass investment opportunities because of the mistaken belief that it takes a lot of money to make a lot of money. What you'll learn in this chapter will prove that this does not have to be the case.

YOU CAN BE A "BIG-TIME" INVESTOR STARTING FROM NEXT TO NIL

If you're talking about returns of six, eight, or ten percent, yes, it does take a lot of money to make a lot of money. But when money doubles, triples, or quadruples in value each year then a little can go a mighty long way. And that's what we'll be discussing here—unusual, sometimes little-known investment opportunities that hold outstanding promise. What these methods have done for others they could very well do for you.

First, though, you have to rid yourself of some conventional thinking about financial investments. There is a so-called investment "rule" that has held far too many people back. This rule states:

In order to earn a great deal of money with an investment, you must assume a great amount of risk.

Not so! Small-risk investments can be just as lucrative, provided you choose the right ones. And that, of course, is what this chapter is all about, discovering low-risk, high-potential opportunities in five investment categories:

1. Investments that produce income
2. Investments that you upgrade in value
3. Investments that are self-multiplying
4. Investments that turn over rapidly
5. Investments that put stock in the future

Investments that involve an element of risk? Certainly all investments do. But throughout our discussion I'll be pointing to ways that can minimize the risks while maximizing your profit opportunities.

HOW $1,500 BUILDS A MULTI-MILLION-DOLLAR PORTFOLIO

Can you still build a fortune starting with $1,500? Ask Veronica F. She's one of the many people who have done it. Her field is apartment houses. Yours may well be something else, but the principles could be much the same.

"I started," Veronica says, "by falling in love with a rather plain-looking three-story wooden structure that had an apartment on each floor. I know that most women fall in love with 'dream houses' and I did, too. Only my dream was to make money with this shabby building.

"I had passed it each day on my way to work at a local laundry. There it sat, begging for some paint and an increase in the rents. This, I was convinced, was Opportunity with a capital 'O.' So one day when the owner tacked a "For Sale" sign on the front, I started to carry out my dream.

"The owner, it seemed, was a widow who was retiring to Florida. She explained to me that ever since her husband had died a decade previously, she had not been able to keep it up. It was really a vicious cycle. The small rents from the three tenants wouldn't pay for upkeep, and she couldn't demand higher rents without improvements to the building.

"She was asking $18,000 for the structure with $5,000 down. I told her I'd pay $16,000 with $4,000 down and she immediately accepted my offer. I gave her $1,000 for an option to buy, the money to be applied to the down payment should I carry out the option.

"Even though I had nothing like $4,000 in ready cash, I knew there would be no problem obtaining the down payment. You see, the building was put up in the days when houses had considerable land surrounding them, and this was no exception. Part of the property was an adjacent lot that would be just right for someone who wanted to build a home. I called on a few real estate brokers and within a week was put in contact with someone who would pay me $4,000 for that lot. So even before I had closed the purchase I had rounded up the entire down payment.

"There was some fast paper shuffling on the day of the closings—with me signing the mortgage, the seller signing the deed, the buyer of the lot turning over $4,000 to me, and me signing the check over to the lady who was moving to Florida. That $4,000 covered the entire down payment, so she returned the original $1,000 option payment I had made. With this amount, and another $500 I took out of the bank, I paid $300 in legal and closing fees, painted the building, installed attractive shutters, and did some minor interior work.

"Then I raised the rents by 25%. This made the building instantly worth 25% more than what I had 'paid' for it, because income property is valued on the basis of how much it earns. The upshot is that I sold the apartment house for $20,000, making $8,000 on a $1,500 investment."

Here's the financial breakdown of what Veronica accomplished:

Purchase price	$16,000
Purchase expenses	300
Total cost	16,300
Amount of mortgage	12,000
Net cost	4,300
Sale of lot	4,000
Net out-of-pocket	300
Improvement costs	1,200
Total personal investment	1,500
Proceeds from sale	20,000
Less mortgage balance	12,000
After-sale cash-on-hand	8,000

Veronica's profit was better than 430% on that deal. And, as you may have guessed, she didn't stop there. That $8,000 was used to buy a larger building. The improvement process was repeated, and repeated again and again, until now she owns buildings valued at several million dollars, providing her with a five-figure monthly income.

Can you repeat Veronica's success? I'll leave that for you to determine after you have been introduced to the Rental Real Estate Fortune Formula, which is just one of the many powerful investment techniques you'll be learning in this chapter.

CATEGORY #1:
INVESTMENTS THAT PRODUCE INCOME

Starting with less than $1,500, you can build a personal gold mine because of two very important factors:

1. A smart investment will bring profits worth many times your initial out-of-pocket cost.
2. The value of the investment itself can be multiplied by re-investing some of the profits. This re-investment will generate even greater profits.

These are the two factors that will guide our selection as we examine outstanding income-producing investments in four fields:

- Equipment Rentals
- Franchises
- Rental Real Estate
- Second Mortgages

Let's look at these four fields individually to learn how others are reaping giant rewards in them, and to examine the rules that will allow you to do the same thing.

Equipment Rentals

As an illustration of how dollars can be self-multiplying in the equipment rental field, consider this: You buy a small travel trailer secondhand for $3,000, place a little ad in the paper offering to rent it on a weekly basis, and actually do rent it for 40 weeks of the year at $100 a week. Your return the first year alone is $4,000. This covers the purchase price, maintenance, and administrative expenses. Each year after that is almost pure gravy. Giving the trailer a useful life of five years, you have taken in $20,000 on an out-of-pocket investment of $3,000. Naturally, long before the five years have expired, you have used some of the profits to acquire more trailers to place in your rental fleet.

It's a highly workable profit formula, and, of course, it is not confined to travel trailers. Consider these possibilities:

Crowd Accommodations: Whenever people gather for a special occasion, special needs have to be met. To meet those needs, enterprising businesspeople rent tents for $150 a day, PA systems for $50 and up, folding chairs for 50¢ each, and even portable toilet structures for $50 each. It's easy to see how these items can quickly pay for themselves and bring you an overly-generous profit.

Office Equipment: For a variety of reasons, including the tax benefits, many business firms prefer to lease their office equipment rather than buy. They also lease when the need will be temporary. That's why you can make excellent money by renting and leasing such items as typewriters, duplicators, copy machines, answering machines, paging systems, background music systems, CB communications equipment, extension telephones, microcomputers, and even desks and chairs.

Tools: Individuals and businesses who need specialized tools on a temporary basis realize that it's a lot wiser to rent than to buy. There are hundreds of tools to choose from, so base your choice on something that is frequently needed in your own area. One of the most common rental items in this category is the floor sander. Others include buffers, ladders, paint-sprayers, backhoes, cement mixers, sandblasters, truck dollies, chainsaws, and air compressors.

Vehicles: We've already discussed trailers, and big money is also being made by those who rent motor homes, boats, pickup trucks, limousines, even golf carts and bicycles. True, some of these items cost well over $1,500 new, but you can cut down on your out-of-pocket investment by (1) buying secondhand, and (2) buying on time.

How to Set Up an Equipment Rental Business

Since our investment ceiling is $1,500, you have the choice of buying one fairly expensive rental item (perhaps on time) or stocking up on an inexpensive item in quantity. Featuring an expensive item such as a trailer means that you are not involved in a lot of individual rental transactions. One customer rents the trailer and your money for the week has been earned. Having a lot of inexpensive items such as floor sanders means you'll be handling many more rental transactions to earn the same amount of money. But, unlike the expensive item, you have plenty to go around—and customers will seldom have to be turned away.

Some rules for equipment rental success:

1. Your initial goal should be to enlarge your starting inventory as soon as possible, paying for it out of profits. Thus, the busi-

ness must be operated from your home or apartment in order to cut down on costs.

2. If your rental item is for the consumer or homeowner, minimize your advertising expense by running small classified ads rather than having display ads or printed brochures. If it's an item that is likely to be rented by businesses or organizations, then contacting them directly (either in person or through a circular) is your most efficient means of drumming up rentals.

3. Feature one—and only one—type of item, at least at the start. Trying to offer floor sanders, paint sprayers, and half a dozen other items all at the same time will spread you too thin. Learn as much as you can about the one type of machine you choose so that you can handle whatever routine maintenance is required. Having a small inventory of spare parts is advisable.

Several years ago, Chet T. bought a large secondhand tent for $1,400. It was attractive, with pink and white candy stripes, and he knew it would be in demand for outdoor gatherings such as weddings, auctions, church socials, lawn parties, and bazaars. Chet's rental fee was $150 a day, and that included setting up and taking down the tent. He soon was averaging two rentals a week, and before the first summer was over he had sufficient profit to pay for buying additional tents.

"My problem was time," Chet recalls. "But I went ahead and bought two additional tents anyway. I made an arrangement with a semi-retired man to handle the tent installations for me. I pay him $50 per rental transaction, which leaves me with $100 and almost no work. The system has been so good that I've now ordered three additional tents—new ones—which I will use for setting up a rental business in another community, again having a local man do the work for one third of the total rental fee."

Franchises

Most people who are considering a full-time major investment business give serious thought to franchises. But people in the under-$1,500 and spare-time category often ignore franchises in the mistaken belief that there are no franchises to fit their needs. The fact is that there are a number of highly workable franchise arrangements that you can obtain with low out-of-pocket investments and run in your spare time.

It's even possible to buy a franchise worth as much as $10,000 with less than $1,500 down, by choosing one in which the parent company—

the franchisor—obtains or provides financing for you. It's part of the package and they offer it to you if they're convinced that you're the right person to run their type of business in your community.

How can you learn of franchise opportunities? There is an excellent listing in the annual *Directory of Franchising Organizations* published by Pilot Industries, 347 Fifth Avenue, New York, NY 10016.

The typical low-cost opportunity? Consider the experience of Fred R., as related in my earlier book, *Second Income Money Makers,* available from Parker Publishing Co., Inc., West Nyack, NY 10994. Fred obtained a franchise featuring burglar alarm systems that he rents to merchants in and around his community. The average system rents for $25 a month, and half of that is pure profit. His rental firm—still a part-time operation—now has about 100 units "on location" and this means that he's clearing $1250 a month.

Rental Real Estate

You've read of the riches earned by Veronica F. through apartment house investments. What she did, in effect, was to follow the Rental Real Estate Fortune Formula:

1. Find a small, well-located apartment house with three or four units. Choose one that is under-priced because it is in need of minor improvements. Make a down payment of 25% or less and take out a mortgage for the remainder.
2. Make improvements—especially those that upgrade the appearance—using your rental income.
3. Increase the rents to match the improved building now enjoyed by the tenants.
4. Either sell the apartment building at its new, higher value based on the increased rents, or refinance the mortgage on the same basis. Use the proceeds to obtain another, larger building.
5. Continue this process of buying, improving, and either selling or refinancing until you reach the kind of wealth category you desire.

As you probably know, one of the great advantages of rental real estate is the fact that you are enjoying the benefits of tremendous financial leverage. Your down payment (and perhaps part of the initial improvement money) is the last cash you personally have to provide. From there on out, the tenants pay for the building.

Let's say, to keep our illustration simple, that you buy one building and hold on to it until the mortgage is paid off. Your initial investment is $1,500. At the time the mortgage is paid off you sell it for $25,000. Not only do you have $23,500 profit (the rental fees having covered operating expenses, taxes, and mortgage payments) but you've also been earning, each year, a generous return on your investment!

There are also great tax advantages. Even though real estate almost always increases in value, the income tax people allow you to treat it as though it were actually declining in value. Part of your profit is written off as depreciation. This puts even more dollars in your pocket.

Second Mortgages

There are still a lot of people with a little cash to invest who avoid second mortgages like the plague, fearful that such investments are not "secure." They've read that the holder of the first mortgage has first call on the money should a foreclosure be necessary, and that holders of second mortgages usually lose out. This will never happen to you if you follow this guideline:

Pick second mortgage situations where the total value of both mortgages (the first and the second) is at least 25% below the true value of the property.

Look at it this way: If the First National Bank has a mortgage on a home worth $25,000, and the balance due on that mortgage is $15,000, it would be entirely reasonable to consider offering a second mortgage in the amount of $1,500. If foreclosure becomes necessary (highly unlikely in such a situation because it would be wiser for the owner to sell the property and pay off the mortgages himself), there is more than enough money to meet both debts.

With first mortgages earning in the 11% category these days (and second mortgages considerably more), there are few investments that are equally profitable, equally conservative, and equally non-demanding of your time. (While rental real estate can bring in a lot more dollars, managing and improving apartment houses does require personal attention; once you've invested in a safe mortgage your only time requirement is the few moments it takes to deposit your monthly checks.)

Is it possible to use leverage in the second mortgage field? Yes, many practitioners do use borrowed funds as their lending capital. It's possible because the rate they receive for second mortgages is well above what they have to pay to obtain the money in the first place. These people are following the same principle that allows banks and other formal lending institutions to stay in business. A bank, after all, is not loaning you its own money; it is loaning you money that it has, in effect, borrowed from other people—money that was placed there by depositors. What works for the long-established professionals can work for you, provided you move just as carefully as they do.

Consider, for example, the experience of Keith M., who got his start in the second mortgage field by lending $1,000 of his own funds and another $1,000 in borrowed money. He knew he was covered because the second mortgage and first mortgage, when added together, were well below the real value of the property.

Keith reports: "I paid 12% for the money I borrowed, and received 16% for the second mortgage, giving me a net profit of 4% on that thousand dollars. Or, looking at it another way, I received 20% return on the thousand dollars that I personally put up."

Why, you ask, would a homeowner agree to pay 16% interest for a second mortgage when he could refinance his existing first mortgage at a lower rate? This occurs when he wants the money for a shorter period of time than is covered by the existing mortgage. The first mortgage may have 20 or more years to run, but he may only want the extra $2,000 or so for six or seven years. He could never afford to pay off the entire mortgage "package" in that short a period, but he could comfortably pay a few thousand that way. In other words, the rate is higher, but the conditions are more agreeable.

Another way to make big money with second mortgages is to purchase existing mortgages at a discount and then collect interest on them as if you had paid the full amount. Quite often, investors will sell their second mortgages to other investors at discounts ranging from 10% off to as much as 50% off the face value. You might, for example, buy a $2,000 mortgage for $1,600. Even though you paid less than the face amount of the mortgage, you receive interest payments based on the full amount.

Full details of this powerful money-making method are included in the fascinating book, *Double Your Money in Six Years: How to Reap Profits in Discounted Mortgages,* by D. Robert Burleigh. It's available from Parker Publishing Company, Inc., West Nyack, N.Y. 10994.

One extremely important point: Don't invest—and even more emphatically, don't make a leveraged investment—until you've carefully studied this field. The rewards can be outstanding, but it does take a lot of initial homework. Make a false move and it can be risky and expensive. Make the right, well-informed moves and it can be a bonanza. My own personal opinion is that it can be a lot safer and a lot more rewarding than such popular investments as land speculation or commodities.

CATEGORY #2:
INVESTMENTS THAT YOU UPGRADE IN VALUE

You can make an investment instantly worth a lot more than what you paid for it by making certain changes or improvements that cost far less than the value enhancement they create. It works like this:

1. You buy an item that is basically good but is in need of a minor fix-up or spruce-up.
2. You perform (or arrange for) the improvements that are needed.
3. You sell the item for its enhanced value.
4. You repeat the process over and over again, specializing, of course, in one type of item in order to function at peak efficiency.

It can be done with inexpensive items (in volume) or with major investments (purchased one at a time). There are only three basic requirements for success in this field:

1. The investment item must be available for purchase in sufficient quantity to make it worthwhile.
2. You must have, or be able to develop, the ability to provide the value enhancement.
3. There must be a sufficient sales market for the value-enhanced product.

In a South Atlantic state, a husband and wife team has used the investment upgrading principle to build a small family fortune. The specialty of Ray and Wendy K. is buying older homes, sprucing them up, and then reselling them for at least 25% more than what they paid. Rarely is their profit less than $5,000 per sale, and often it's much more.

Ray and Wendy, working in their spare time nights and weekends, average about six buy-improve-resell transactions each year. In a recent year they cleared more than $50,000.

"The kind of home we look for," Ray explains, "is one that is in a good location, but which has not been kept as well as its neighboring homes. Then what we do is provide the paint, siding, minor landscaping, or whatever might be needed to bring it up to par with the neighboring homes."

The couple explains that the location of the home is much more important to them than the condition. "We can improve the condition," Wendy notes, "but there is nothing we can do to improve the location. And it's amazing what a paint job costing only a few hundred dollars can do to enhance the resale value. The very first house we bought was a basically sound structure that needed only a coat of paint and new linoleum in the kitchen. We paid $20,000 for it, spent $475 for materials, did the work ourselves, and sold the home for $27,500 within four months."

Although initially Ray and Wendy did all of the work themselves, they now find it more profitable to hire out much of it. This way they can handle several homes at the same time, thus increasing their profit potential.

That first home, purchased for $20,000, was obtained with a $4,000 down payment. Ray and Wendy put up $1,000 of their own cash and got the other $3,000 by increasing the mortgage on their own personal home. The profit enabled them to pay back the $3,000 on their personal mortgage and gave them money for down payments on two additional houses to buy, improve, and resell.

Examine These Other Buy-Improve-Resell Possibilities

There's a big field to choose from if you decide that investment upgrading is for you. Remember, though, that items with a resale value of less than $75 or $100 will generally not provide enough profit to make the effort worthwhile. Here's a proven fact:

The higher the basic value of the item, the more profit you can make with each dollar of improvement you provide.

Consider as an example Ray and Wendy's first house. Taking brokerage and interest costs into account, and rounding out the figures, let's say that they spent $500 on improvements and cleared $6,000 on the deal. This means that they earned $12 for each dollar spent. Now let's imagine that instead of homes they had chosen tricycles as their specialty, buying the trikes for $5, spending $3 to improve them, and selling them for $12.50. Here, their return is only $1.50 for each dollar spent on improvements. It's also interesting to note that each dollar earned on cheaper items such as tricycles requires more work than on items of higher value.

So, with a $75-$100 minimum in mind, let's take a look at some of the investment upgrading possibilities open to you. Naturally, I can't present a complete list but these examples will serve to spur your own thinking. Already having discussed the older house category, we'll omit that field from the listing.

Airplanes. Private flying is a highly popular avocation, and many pilots are in the market for used planes. A New Jersey resident specializes in buying damaged aircraft, salvaging the usable components, and using those parts to put together highly saleable airplanes.

Antique cars. Many hobbyists are looking for antique cars that they can restore, and, of course, such vehicles are becoming a lot harder to find. So a Californian buys parts of antique cars—a chassis here, headlamps there, etc.—and puts them together until he has enough for a complete car. He sells the newly-assembled units "as is," ready for the buyer to apply elbow grease, paint, and loving care.

Antique Radios. Thousands of attics and junk shops contain non-working radios that were manufactured 40 or more years ago. By collecting spare parts from some and installing them in others, you have the basis of a highly profitable business catering to collectors.

Business Machines. Many small business firms, and some larger ones, recognize the economy that can be achieved by purchasing rebuilt rather than new office equipment. A Michigan man specializes in trade-ins. He allows his business customers to trade in machines for rebuilt ones. Then he spruces up the trade-ins to sell to somebody else

Clocks. Old mechanical clocks, including those with works made entirely of wood, are in great demand by collectors. Buy everything in this category that you can find—as an Ohio lady does—assemble fully functional timepieces out of the parts you have obtained, and you'll find purchasers trying to break down your door.

Pianos. Have you priced a new piano recently? If you have, then you know why used spinets, uprights, and grands are in such demand. You can learn how to tune, repair, and refinish these items from a home study course (check the mechanics magazines for home study ads) and then double or triple your money each time you make a transaction.

Pump Organs. There are still thousands of these around, to be found mostly in older homes. A relative of mine travels to rural areas buying up these items at auctions (and also by placing "Items Wanted" ads in weekly newspapers), takes them to his basement workshop, patches whatever needs patching, and sells them at considerable profit. Heavy to lug? Yes, but a utility trailer and a two-wheel dolly make it much easier.

CATEGORY #3
INVESTMENTS THAT ARE SELF-MULTIPLYING

Buy and sell living things with Mother Nature as your partner and you have an investment that just has to grow. Here's an example from my files:

Gene F. lives on a five-acre plot about 50 miles from New York City. Deciding that he'd like to earn some money from that land with a minimum amount of work, Gene sent to a mail order nursery and ordered several hundred tiny evergreen trees for pennies each. He then placed them in the soil on part of his property, and hired a local high school boy to stop by occasionally and keep the section free of weeds.

"I repeated that process each year," Gene recalls, "setting out several hundred seedlings each time. Then, in a very few years the original group had reached a few feet in height and I put a sign out front announcing that I had evergreens for sale on a 'dig-your-own' basis. The prices were well below what anyone would have to pay a commercial nursery, and I sold the trees for at least ten times what I had invested in them. I'm now selling an average of 500 trees a year to homeowners who want them to landscape their grounds or who want to cut them as Christmas trees—and I can't think of a better 'growth' investment."

In another example from my files, Joe H. borrowed $5,000 from a friend and became a back yard vintner. The wine produced from his vines is now sold across much of the country. It started out as a family project, and is now aided by some hired help. Joe regularly turns down multi-million dollar offers from big producers who'd like to buy him out.

I could give you dozens of other examples in such fields as:

Angora Rabbits	Guinea Pigs
Chinchillas	Guppies
Exotic Animals	Herbs
Fish Bait	Maple Syrup
Fruit	Mushrooms

Orchids	Purebred Dogs
Pheasants	Siamese Cats
Pigeons	Songbirds
Pond-bred Trout	Squab
Ponies	Timber

It's important to remember that Mother Nature doesn't do all of the work. She takes care of the reproduction and growth processes for you, but there's some nurturing to be done by you or by people you hire. Any of the items on the list can be handled in your spare time, and you can select a type of item to fit the size of your home or property. There's at least one item on the list for just about anybody's circumstances.

CATEGORY #4:
INVESTMENTS THAT TURN OVER RAPIDLY

One factor that prevents many people from making investments is the fear that their money will be tied up indefinitely. Buying rural land on speculation can, for example, involve a wait of several years or more before the price appreciates to the point where a profitable sale can be made.

And while your money is tied up in an investment, you are unable to put it into other investments. That's why a number of shrewd investors put their dollars into items that are guaranteed to turn over rapidly. What kind of items? Collector's items—things that collectors are anxious to get hold of.

The secret, of course, is to get the items before the collectors do— and get them cheaply enough to provide you with a substantial profit. I'll let you in on the secret that will allow you to accomplish this with such items as:

Antique Firearms	Old Dolls
Antique Furniture	Phonograph Records
Autographs	Prints
Coins	Rare Books
Comic Books	Stamps
Old Bottles	Works of Art

The above, as you can see, is a list of highly popular collector's items. I could have included many more, but you get the idea. Now let me give you Rule Number One:

You are an investor, not a speculator. Don't even consider things that you think might become collector's items in the future. Buy only what is <u>already</u> in the collector's item category.

This way, you know there is big demand for the items you buy and resell. You are guaranteed a quick turnover so that you can then put your money into additional items for resale, keeping your dollars continuously working for you.

And now for the secret that will let you get collector's items in your chosen field sooner and cheaper than private collectors can obtain them:

Buy entire lots—the bad with the good.

That's the secret, pure and simple. Just eight words, but those eight words virtually guarantee success. To demonstrate this powerful principle in action, I'll relate the experience of Gil T., whose specialty is old firearms. He runs ads in a number of regional newspapers seeking firearms to purchase and announcing that he has firearms for sale.

"When people call and say they have one or two guns for sale, I tell them to bring them in for me to appraise. Occasionally I make a good purchase that way," Gil reports, "but my really profitable buys are when people are disposing of their collections and have a dozen or more pieces for sale.

"When that happens, I move quickly. I go to the person's home to inspect the items. Most of the time only about 10% of the items are really in the collector's item category. The owner knows this, and has priced them rather high. I offer to buy the entire lot—the good with the bad—at a reasonable price.

"The owner knows that if other collectors were to come in, they would snap up the good items and leave him with the remainder unsold. My offer actually provides him with more money than he would otherwise receive, and I carefully explain this to the owners who don't already understand it.

"So what I do is take everything off his hands, sell the routine items for about what I paid for them, and achieve a hefty markup on the pieces that are in the collector category. This gives me access to some of the best collector's items in my part of the country."

The same principle employed by Gil with firearms will work with just about any other type of collector's item—from old bottles to works of art. Naturally, you must be knowledgeable in whatever field you choose. Having been an avid collector yourself is a good basis from which to start. From that point, the most important thing to learn is how to set the prices you will pay.

Here's Gil's formula:

Pay 55% of the retail value of the items you really want, and close to the full retail value of the routine items that you will sell for approximate cost.

This gives you true collector's items at nearly half off. Even accounting for the administrative expense of buying, moving, and selling the "remainders" you are left with a substantial profit on the higher-priced, true collector's items.

One more tip from Gil. Never tell the person from whom you are buying what you are paying for each individual item. Give him one price—the price for the entire lot.

CATEGORY #5:
INVESTMENTS THAT PUT STOCK IN THE FUTURE

At the outset of this chapter I promised you we would deal only with low-risk investments. I intend to expand on that promise by showing how you can take much of the speculation out of speculative investments.

Take stocks as an example. Speculating in the stock market is described as something only for the rich or daring, and at the same time we are told that only the speculators stand to make any really big profits in the market.

Is there such a thing, then, as low-risk speculation? Yes indeed, and you achieve it by spreading the risk. It's as old as not putting all your apples in the same basket and as new as cashing in on the modern wave of stock profits: calls and puts.

What are calls and puts? They are options to buy or sell stocks at some stated point in the future. You don't actually buy or sell the stock—at least not initially—you merely pay someone for the right to do so.

When you buy a call, you enter into a contract with the owner of a certain stock. He agrees to sell you his stock at a specified price any time within the period of the contract. The price stated in the call is, naturally, higher than the price for which the stock is currently selling. Why, then, would you buy a call? Because you expect the stock to rise in price.

If it is worth $50 now and you expect it to rise to $75 in several months, you might buy a call. Then, if it does rise in price, you exercise the call, buying the stock for $50 per share and immediately selling it on the open market for its real value.

A put is just the opposite. Instead of agreeing to sell you a stock at a certain price, a put dealer agrees to buy it from you at the specified price. You don't even have to own it at the time you enter into the contract. You buy a put when you expect a certain stock to drop dramatically in price. If this happens within the time period specified in the contract, you exercise the put—buying the stock on the open market for the current price and immediately selling it to the put dealer at the higher price specified in your contract.

Two big advantages

You may wonder why it wouldn't be wiser merely to deal in the stock directly. If, for example, you expect a stock to rise, why not just go out and buy it? There are two reasons: leverage and spreading the risk.

Calls generally sell for 10%-15% of the current price of the stock they cover. Thus, if Witt Amalgamated is selling for $50 per share and you expect it to rise, you can get in on the action for $500 or $750. This gives you the right to buy 100 shares for $50 each at any time within the next, say, six months. Then if the stock rises to $75 per share, you exercise your option, buying the shares for $5,000 and immediately turning around and selling them for $7,500. Your initial investment of $500 or $750 has brought you a $2,500 profit. If, on the other hand, you had actually bought the stock instead of an option—and had actually paid $5,000 for it—your profit would be far less per dollar invested.

Options make spreading the risk possible because their lower cost enables you to invest in a wider range of stock issues. Your investment "apples" are in a lot of baskets. Let's say that only one out of three calls actually pays off. You've lost $750 on each of the calls that didn't pan out because the stock failed to rise in price. You tear up the two options and lose any hope of recovering the $1,500. But the third option does pan out. You make $3,000 on that particular deal. Thus, taking all three investments into account, you have still made $1,500.

I've given you just the bare basics of how the options market works. You'll need to learn a lot more. But this you can easily do because reams of informative literature are available. It's become such a popular and effective type of investment that three times as many options are being sold today than were being sold ten years ago.

How do you get started? Check the brokers who advertise regularly in the financial pages. Request literature. Go to the bookstore or library and obtain a book or two on the subject. It will be fascinating reading, and it could just mark the financial turning point in your life.

12

Sell Your Skills

Too many people search far and wide for new ways to make money when they already have, within themselves, the ability to make all the money they want and need. They ignore the advice of Longfellow, who said: "The talent of success is nothing more than doing what you can do well, and doing well whatever you do."

In the course of your hobbies, pastimes, work experience, and everyday living you have developed some highly useful talents and abilities. Don't be turned off by the fact that many other people share these aptitudes. Most of them don't know what you are about to learn—the secret of converting a common skill into an abundant source of income.

We're going to take 30 skills (or, in some cases, simply areas of personal interest) and demonstrate how any one of them can become the basis of a highly successful business that you can launch inexpensively and run in your spare time. In this list there certainly will be several items that match your own abilities and interests.

BASE A BUSINESS ON WHAT COMES NATURALLY

Why take the time and trouble to learn a new trade when you can earn plenty of money doing what comes naturally? Apply a skill you already have and you can begin earning right away. And because you'll be doing what you enjoy, the rewards will be more than financial.

Don't worry about competition. You won't be selling your skills in the usual way. You won't be following the crowd by trying to peddle commonplace skills to an already overcrowded market. Instead, you'll be selling to an entirely different market, one that you have created for yourself.

That, in fact, is the key to all of the techniques outlined in this chapter. It involves providing a unique product or service that puts you far ahead of other people who are trying to make money in the same general field as you. Consider as an example the experience of a carpenter friend of mine.

HOW $350 STARTS A $600-PER-WEEK BUSINESS

Seth K. is a good carpenter, but even good carpenters have trouble finding work during seasonal and economic declines in the construction industry. This is what caused him to seek a means of supplementing his income.

His first thought, naturally, was to seek temporary jobs doing remodeling work for homeowners and businessmen, but because of all the other carpenters in the same boat there wasn't enough work to go around.

"It seemed that everybody who knew how to handle a hammer and saw was out there fighting for work and beating me to the punch," he remembers. "So the only thing left for me to do was to create work of my own."

And that's precisely what he did. If all the available work was taken, why not set himself up as a specialist in a certain type of carpentry and then show people how badly they needed his type of work done?

I'll tell you what his specialty is, although it doesn't really matter. He could have chosen any of a dozen lines and have been equally successful simply because he wasn't just out there grabbing whatever he could get. He was creating a need in the minds of his customers and then filling it.

His specialty is homes-for-sale. He doesn't buy them and he doesn't sell them. What he does is inspect every home he can find with a "For Sale" sign on it and then demonstrate to the owner how certain repairs and minor changes can enhance its sale value.

"One home that had been on the market for a year without selling did sell shortly after I modernized the kitchen and added some closet space. The Realtor was so impressed that he's recommended me to many of his other clients. Thanks to word-of-mouth from satisfied customers, I haven't been idle a day since I decided on this specialty."

It cost Seth $350 for the advance purchase of materials needed on his first job, and that's all he spent to set himself up in business. He's now averaging $600 a week in what has become his full-time occupation of making homes more saleable.

What Seth did with carpentry you can do with whatever your skill or special area of interest happens to be. The secret lies in creating a new market for your chosen line of work. The great thing about it is that when you create the market, it's practically all yours. Others may eventually spot your success and try to imitate it, but by then you've had a head start and are well established.

HOW TO SELECT YOUR OWN SPECIALTY

You're about to see a comprehensive listing that outlines many of the common skills that can become the basis of a "create-your-own-market" type of business. But, frankly, you probably already know which of your skills to utilize. It should be a skill that:

- You handle easily and well
- You enjoy
- Does not require a big investment in tools or equipment

If you follow these three criteria when considering the business opportunities described in this chapter, you'll be able to start making money almost immediately in a business that's easy to start, fun to run, and expandable to meet your highest income goals.

88 "NEW MARKET" BUSINESS IDEAS TO CHOOSE FROM

Here are 30 common skills and areas of interest, each followed by one or more examples (88 in all) of how "new market" techniques can be used to build that skill or interest into a thriving business. You can learn a lot from each of the categories in the listing, even if it does not match one of your own interests. Seeing how new markets are created for one type of skill can give you valuable ideas for cashing in on your own chosen field.

Animals: Most people who want to base a business on their love of animals think of breeding, selling, or training them. But in a major Midwestern city, one entrepreneur created his own new market by helping to find them. He maintains a registry of lost-

and-found pets. People call his office to report losing or finding an animal. He makes a tape recording of that information which can be heard by anyone who dials a special number he has set aside for that purpose. His profit comes from commercial spot announcements that precede the lost-and-found listing.

Antiques: If your area is already saturated with antique shops, then you need a new market technique to draw business. Instead of selling a conglomeration of antiques, specialize in one type of item, buying and selling nothing else. People get to know that you are the first person to see when they're in the market for something in your line. For example: a New Yorker buys, restores, and sells antique clocks; a Minnesotan specializes in old wagon wheels; a Connecticut couple fills their home shop with nothing but old lamps.

Camping: A lot of stores sell camping supplies, but few rent them. Renting makes sense because most campers use their equipment for only a week or two, or perhaps an occasional weekend. A Massachusetts man started with relatively inexpensive items such as knapsacks, tents, and cooking gear. He's since expanded his line to include travel trailers and camper tops for pickup trucks.

Carpentry· You've already read about Seth K.'s accomplishments in this field. Some other new market ways to make money in carpentry include buying and refurbishing rundown homes before placing them on the market again; producing unfinished furniture of a higher quality than the knotty pine junk so commonly available; making prefabricated doghouses or tool sheds ready for the homeowner to assemble.

Cars: If you love to tinker with cars, here's an excellent way to make money with your hobby: Do driveway tune-ups and oil changes. Many people find it inconvenient to take their car to the garage for servicing. Spare them that task by going to the car instead of having the car come to you and you should find plenty of business. Put your tools in your own van or station wagon and you can handle most routine servicing chores at the customer's location. An added advantage over the regular service station is that you avoid a lot of overhead such as rent, heat, electricity, and insurance.

Children: You love children and they seem to love you, but you don't want to go so far as opening a nursery school or a summer day camp. Well, you can create a new market opportunity in any of several ways: Arrange children's party entertainment; produce semi-educational assembly programs for schools; become a child photographer; put together a mobile nature or science show that travels to shopping centers in a travel trailer and then charge for admission; conduct educational field trips; or, as a New Jersey lady does, you can be a Saturday afternoon movie escort, taking smallfry to the movies and then returning them home when the show is over.

Contests: If you're addicted to contests, and even if you're good at it, you've discovered that the odds are against you because that's the way it's supposed to be. Well, you can win consistently with contests by moving over to the other side. Instead of entering contests, create them and then sell them to local merchants for promotional purposes. In the Philadelphia area, a young housewife earns $20,000 a year in her spare time by thinking up new contests and then running them for her businessmen clients.

Conversation: Being good at conversation qualifies you for a lot of different money-making ventures. The first thing most people think of is selling, but since we're discussing new market opportunities we'll look to some other possibilities, such as conducting public opinion polls, conducting guided tours, coordinating and taking part in a speakers' bureau or handling public relations for charitable organizations and commercial firms. A woman in California runs an unusual form of telephone answering service. Her clients include a number of mail order firms. Any complaint calls they receive are immediately switched to her phone; she deals politely and efficiently with the callers, promising that the complaint will be looked into and that they will receive a reply by postcard. She then compiles each day's list of complaints for each of the clients to deal with. They find her service more efficient and less costly than if each company had to maintain its own complaint desk.

Cooking: New market possibilities in the cooking field include compiling and publishing community recipe booklets featuring the favorite recipes of many of the community's housewives; producing, in volume, desserts for area restaurants; delivering meals-to-order to the workers in business and commercial districts; stationing a hot dog wagon, not alongside a highway, but near athletic and other community events that draw large crowds; selling non-perishable local food specialties through the mail.

Dieting: What can you do for dieters that isn't already being done by a lot of other people? Obviously, diet classes are ruled out. But how about sponsoring group trips to weight-reduction resorts? Or launching a diet book club? Or opening a salad bar restaurant? Or sponsoring one-day diet seminars in various locations? This last idea is borrowed from a New York City woman who travels across the country giving seminars in hotel and motel meeting rooms, charging attendees $15 each for the lecture, a "demonstration" luncheon featuring diet foods, and a follow-up booklet to help them carry on the methods she preaches. Chapter 7 of this book tells how you can set up your own seminar business.

Driving: New market opportunities for people who enjoy driving include providing a chauffeur-driven limousine service; transporting suburbanites to and from city theaters; running a cut-rate children's taxi service for busy parents; conducting historical tours of your area; and coordinating an auto transportation service for people who are moving or planning to spend several months in a vacation spot distant from their home.

Electronics: The average person who is skilled in electronics and who wants to establish a spare-time business thinks first of TV repair. There is more money and less hassle, however, in such new market opportunities as installing and/or servicing commercial communications equipment, small business computers, answering machines, paging systems, internal telephone systems, background music systems, word processors, electronic signs, closed circuit TV setups, and burglar and fire alarm systems. Pick one of these specialties and you'll find far less competition than in TV repairs. And because you're working in a highly specialized field serving businesses instead of individuals you can charge a lot more for your time.

English Language: Later in our listing we'll take a look at writing, but in the present category we're considering ways in which you can help other people with their English. Let's say you've thought of such routine services as tutoring and correcting term papers and ruled them out. Then consider creating your own new market by doing any of the following: coach foreign-born businessmen and professionals to help them get rid of their accents; handle the correspondence of visiting foreign businessmen; proofread manuscripts for publishers; compile indexes for authors; run a résumé service for job-seekers in one or more of the professions. In California, a free-lance writer has developed a lucrative sideline by correcting product instruction booklets prepared by foreign manufacturers. If you've ever seen the awkwardly-worded instructions accompanying certain products from Japan or Taiwan, you understand why his service is so badly needed.

Foreign Languages: Fluency in one or more foreign languages can make money for you in a lot more ways than merely teaching or translating. If you like to travel, you can represent American firms overseas. If you're a stay-at-home, then consider these possibilities: Run a bookstore or mail order book service dealing only in books of another language; serve as a Welcome Wagon-type host or hostess in areas where many foreign-born people reside; operate an employment service for non-native Americans; teach vocational courses to persons who are not fluent in English.

Games: Maybe you're not another Robert Darrow and maybe you don't have a modern-day version of Monopoly up your sleeve. It would be hard to beat that all-time game best-seller. But that doesn't mean that game manufacturers have given up. They're always on the lookout for new game ideas. If you have one or more that you think would sell, first apply for a patent and then start to get in touch with the manufacturers. You'll find their names and addresses on the box covers of the games that fill any department store's toy department. Today's biggest new market opportunity is electronic games based on calculator or microcomputer-like circuits. In fact, some of today's top-selling electronic games are little more than calculators with special functions built in.

Gardening: The standard way to make money in gardening is to sell the produce you grow. Here are some of the new market methods: Rent garden space to apartment dwellers who have no land of their own; start a farmer's market (but in this case for other gardeners) combining their produce so that it can all be sold at one location; build a hothouse and rent space in it to garden hobbyists; breed and sell houseplants; run a houseplant-sitting service for vacationers; run a houseplant or garden clinic for people with non-green thumbs.

Handcrafts: If you feel that producing your own handcrafted items won't make enough money for you, then the answer lies in combining the work of many handcraftsmen. You can promote handcraft shows at local armories or college fieldhouses; sell handcrafted items on commission at flea markets; rent workshop space to hobbyists without shops of their own; buy and sell equipment required for the various crafts; go on a lecture tour demonstrating your own handcraft expertise; or even establish a speakers' bureau featuring a number of experts in various fields. Still another possibility would be to publish a newsletter for people throughout the country who share your hobby. Subscribers can be solicited through small ads in hobby magazines.

Handwriting: Can handwriting possibly be a money-making field? It is for a Chicago woman whose specialty is analyzing the handwriting of job applicants. She does it on behalf of a number of Chicago-based corporations whose personnel departments believe that handwriting analysis helps them to hire good employees. Also worth considering is the fact that graphologists do well financially when they set themselves up in booths at fairs, resort areas, shopping malls, and other areas where people congregate. If, on the other hand, your specialty is your own excellent penmanship rather than the scribblings of others, you can make money in such fields as engraving and calligraphy. Your work can be handled through jewelry shops and printing firms.

Hunting and Fishing: You are probably familiar with the fishing excursion boats that take groups of sportsmen out for the day. But perhaps you haven't heard of this new market technique that is beginning to catch on in several areas: chartered buses or motor homes which take hunters to proven hunting grounds for weekends and longer periods. One entrepreneur in this field uses a former school bus to transport hunters to the mountains, where they are put up in motel rooms he has reserved for them. Then he serves as their guide to the area. Another man, this one the owner of a motor home, takes smaller groups and lodges them right in the vehicle. If fishing is your field but you are not anxious to become a charter boat captain, you can still make money by setting up fishing excursions by bus and taking groups of people to the dock where a boat you have chartered awaits them.

Interior Decorating: Are too many interior decorators in your area concentrating on homes and apartments? You can create your own new market by specializing in commercial assignments. Stores, offices, and restaurants are also in need of professional decorating services. The most successful practitioners are those who specialize in just one of these three fields and build up a reputation in that particular type of work.

Investigating: Dealing with white collar crime is one of the biggest new markets for people skilled in investigative procedures. Many retired policemen used to set themselves up as jack-of-all-trades detectives. Now the ambitious ones know that internal corporate security is the field that offers the greatest financial rewards. Most larger corporations have their own investigating teams, so concentrate on medium-sized and smaller companies.

Mixing Drinks: Many people work as part-time bartenders, taking whatever work they can get—which means that many of them labor in sleazy bars late at night. Raise your sights a bit and consider these new market opportunities: Start a catering service for companies planning receptions and cocktail parties; run a temporary bartenders' service and send other people out to those late-at-night jobs; buy or lease an abandoned restaurant and convert it into a catering hall for wedding receptions, office parties, and club affairs; become a regional representative for one of the many small wineries that are unable to do much promoting of their own products.

Music: If music is your first love but you've ruled out performing and teaching as money-making possibilities, you still have a lot of opportunities to choose from. Among them, you might sponsor chartered bus trips to performances at the nearest concert hall or opera house; produce local concerts by accomplished musicians; arrange guided tours of some of the musical capitals of the world; serve as a booking agent and business manager for fledgling rock groups and dance bands; equip and operate a recording studio for making demo records on behalf of singers, groups, and songwriters.

Office Skills: There are many women in the home typing business, but you can do them one better in this new market opportunity: individually typed form letters. When a business firm needs to send the same letter to many people on its customer or prospect list—but wants the letter individually typed and addressed personally to the recipient—it assigns the work to you. And you do the work at considerably less cost than if the letters were really individually typed. How? By using an automatic typewriter or word processor. While these machines cost several thousand dollars to buy, they can be leased for about $200 a month and sometimes less. Just a few work assignments per month covers your lease cost, and anything over that is gravy. You can also handle billing and bookkeeping with leased microcomputer equipment.

Photography: There are thousands, perhaps even millions, of people skilled in photography, and almost as many would like to be able to make money using this skill. To beat the competition you've got to create your own market by picking a specialty no one else has latched on to. Chapter 10 lists a number of ideas in the new market category. An additional possibility is portraits of pets. The same type of person who buys a cemetery plot for his deceased Fido or Tabby is a leading prospect for a photographic portrait of his pets while they are in the prime of life.

Public Speaking: Today's method of making a good living through public speaking (other than seminars, as outlined in Chapter 7) is to become an advocate. It matters little what you advocate, as long as the "cause" has a number of followers. You make money at it by forming a non-profit organization and getting yourself appointed as its executive director, or public advocate, or public relations director. Naturally, you can't be a hypocrite. You must really believe in the cause. But there's no law—legal, moral, or otherwise—to say that you can't make money by speaking publicly on what you believe in. I'm not being overly cynical when I say that a fair proportion of the do-good groups active in the United States today wouldn't be able to do nearly as much good if it weren't for their highly-paid executives and public-speaking advocates.

Reading: The ability to read well is highly underrated. Some good readers are making money by recording books and magazine articles on cassette tapes for busy people to listen to while they are driving or otherwise occupied; recording radio commercials for business firms; narrating sales films and documentaries; recording sales messages for use over department store PA systems. Have you ever walked into a department store or discount house and heard a sloppy and disconcerting sales pitch interrupt the canned music? A friend of mine capitalized on that and set himself up in business by contracting with a number of stores and chains to visit each store once a week and record sales messages for use during the next seven days. He does a professional job and it has resulted in increased sales for the stores. Another company I know of has arranged tie-ins with the manufacturers of products sold in the various stores; here, the manufacturers pay for product "commercials" that are beamed throughout each store.

Self Defense: The commercial teaching of self defense is usually done in a "school" operated in a rented storefront. From what I've seen, most of these schools fail rapidly. There just isn't a sufficiently large market to allow most of them to meet their overhead costs. Here's a new market opportunity that doesn't require much overhead. Instead of running a storefront school, sell your self defense teaching skills by contract, on location, to business firms. What an Illinois woman has done provides a perfect example. Many companies in her area employ women late at night, and a lot of these women have reason to fear being assaulted while going to or leaving work. Recognizing this, a number of companies have hired this expert in self defense to share some of her knowledge and techniques with female employees. The classes are conducted at each plant over a several-week period, with follow-up sessions held periodically so that the employees' newly-acquired skills are not lost.

Sewing: The heroine of many an old-time novel was the seamstress who labored long hours with needle and thread using her meager wages to help put her children through college. Women who take in sewing today still don't earn very much, and that's because they are not aware of new market opportunities such as making banners and pendants that are needed for store openings and sales, political campaigns, athletic teams, conventions, public celebrations of all types, marching band groups, advertising campaigns, sports tournaments, trade shows, and many other purposes. A classified ad in the Yellow Pages plus some personal contact with ad agencies in your area should provide you with a lot of highly remunerative work.

Travel: Is travel a skill? Yes, if you've found ways to make it easier, less expensive, or more interesting. A Long Island man has earned a small fortune by putting out little books that contain money-saving travel tips. Many people combine travel with other special interests by conducting tours to areas that are important to those special interests; hence there are art tours, opera tours, historical tours, religious tours, and even wine tours. If you don't want to arrange and conduct tours yourself, you can sell prepackaged tours that are offered by a number of nationally-known companies. You sign up 30 or 40 people and then keep a percentage of the gross. The tour packages are advertised regularly in the professional travel magazines available in many larger libraries.

Writing: Your first novel didn't sell? And your second and your third? Couldn't even sell a joke to Reader's Digest? Don't despair. You were merely trying to do what hundreds of thousands of other people are attempting to do. With all the competition, the odds against making a major sale are tremendous. But a lot of smaller sales can add up to much more money than one major one, believe it or not. There are thousands of magazines in the United States that you never heard of. These are trade and special interest publications that cater to small, select groups. They pay from $100 to $500 for an article, and if you know your field well enough you can bang out an article in an hour or two. To make good money serving this new market, you must specialize. Pick a field of knowledge and learn all you can about it. Then start writing. The most successful trade magazine writers I know have specialties that are of interest to many different publications. This means that instead of specializing in, say, the manufacture of corrugated boxes they specialize in something like the techniques of photographing a product well. This means that similar articles can be sold to many different magazines rather than just to a trade publication in the corrugated box field.

A STEP-BY-STEP GUIDE TO
THE SUCCESSFUL MARKETING OF YOUR SKILLS

A thorough reading of each of the categories in the above listing has given you a good idea of many of the novel and effective means that can be used to create a new market for everyday skills. Even if your own chosen skill was not included in the listing, you've gained some excellent insights into how it can be marketed. Methods that work well in promoting one skill often work equally well in an entirely different line.

But now let's be more specific. Let's spell out the four-step program that will set you up in a profitable and growing business:

1. Examine the market potential.
2 Equip yourself to serve the market.
3. Create your marketing plan.
4. Expand with OPL and OPM.

We'll examine each of these steps individually, demonstrating how each has worked for others and can be equally effective for you.

STEP #1:
Examine the Market Potential

Before a new market can be created, there must be a potential for it. How do you examine the market potential? You might do as Barbara W. did and offer your planned service or product to a few selected prospects and wait for the response.

Barbara's idea was to lease a word processing machine and turn out personal "form" letters for businessmen. (See the Office Skills category in the new market listing.) She did not, however, want to sign a 12-month lease for the needed equipment until she knew that there was a market for her service.

Her solution was to type, on her own non-automatic typewriter, some letters that she sent to a number of executives in her city. She pointed out the advantage of individually-typed letters when sent to customers and prospects.

"And then," Barbara reports, "I informed each of the executives that I could prepare any number of similarly-worded letters for them at far less cost than if they were to have their own typists do the work. I stressed that the typing would be error free and that the letters could even contain a personal reference or two geared to each recipient, thanks to my word processing setup.

"As a clincher, I suggested that they include a word-processed letter along with the next batch of bills they sent out to their customers. I pointed out that the letter would be good public relations and could even increase business by mentioning some new products or services offered by the company."

The response Barbara received was a definite indication that a market existed for her product.

"You can bet," she says, "that I quickly signed the lease for that word processing machine!" Her business has grown to the point where she now has three machines banging out letters full-time.

One of the most effective techniques of examining the market potential for a new product or service idea is to actually test the idea. Offer it in the marketplace and wait for the response. Naturally, you must be prepared to provide the offered service or product. If initial tests don't prove conclusive and you want to do more testing before obtaining the needed equipment and supplies, you can "farm" out any initial assignments you receive as a result of your test advertising.

STEP #2:
Equip Yourself to Serve the Market

Because you are basing your business on a skill you already have, you may already possess all or most of the needed equipment. Such was the case with Larry R., who runs a driveway tune-up service in the Northeast.

"I'd been a back yard mechanic for years," Larry explains, "and had accumulated more than enough tools to handle tune-ups and oil changes in customers' driveways. The only thing I needed was a van to haul the stuff around in, and I found a serviceable vehicle at a nearby used car lot."

In some cases, however, the equipment required by the business may go well beyond what you already have on hand. For years, Bart G. had been taking friends on hunting trips to a New England state. Each year more friends wanted to join the party.

"And when friends of friends began to want in, I realized I had a potential gold mine," Bart recalls. "But for the business to be profitable, I'd have to take a lot of people at once. What did I do? I went out and bought a used school bus. Not the most comfortable bus in the world, but it served the purpose. I arranged with a motel in the hunting area to reserve rooms for all members of each party I drove up there."

Hunting being seasonal, the business is still part-time. But Bart, who is now retired from his regular job, makes more money in his hunting excursion enterprise than he receives from the generous pension provided by his former employer.

Larry, in his driveway tune-up business, and Bart, in his hunting excursion enterprise, both avoided a mistake that is made by far too many people starting out in business. They did not over-equip themselves. It's a common error to buy newer, better, or more expensive equipment than you need to get the business started. This leaves you with less cash for working capital in the early days of your venture.

You should follow this rule:

Start your skill-based business on as small a scale as you can with the minimum amount of equipment that will allow you to do the job well.

Once your business has been launched and begins to return a profit you'll be in a far better position to determine precisely what additional equipment you need to provide the venture with continued growth.

STEP #3:
Create a Marketing Plan

When you are selling a product or service to what is essentially a new market your marketing plan has to differ somewhat from the way other people sell similar skills to an existing market. Seth K., the carpenter you met earlier in this chapter, did not advertise his services in the Yellow Pages or in any newspaper classified listing, as most carpentry businesses do. He was catering to a special person—the home-seller—and so he contacted his potential customer directly, pointing out alterations he could provide that would make the home more saleable.

Judy W., the young housewife who creates contests for merchants, found regular advertising to be of little help.

"I was introducing what amounted to a new idea to many of the merchants," she explains, "and few, if any, of them would be likely to call me up and say 'Hey, Judy, how about doing a contest for me?' I had to show each of them how a contest could bring a lot more people into his or her store, and how the cost of the contest would be more than offset by increased business volume. How did I do this? I got myself invited to service club and Chamber of Commerce meetings, and I made a presentation that persuaded many of them to sign up."

This doesn't mean that you should always rule out normal channels of advertising. It simply means that since you are creating a new market, you should put more emphasis on convincing people of the need for the type of product or service you offer. Then the business will naturally flow to you because (1) it was you who spelled out the need, and (2) there's little if any competition.

Computer crime is a growing worry for many American businesses, and Victor A. has been able to use normal business advertising channels to sell his computer security service. Vic is a former computer programmer who spotted a new market in creating special programs to prevent unauthorized persons from gaining access to computers. He advertises in publications geared to the data processing market. His service is unusual, he is one of the few people to have become specialists in the field, and he has all the business he can handle.

STEP #4:
Expand with OPL and OPM

If there is any drawback to businesses based on personal skills, it is that you are seemingly limited to whatever you can personally produce. I say "seemingly" because the limitation doesn't really exist. Other

People's Labor and Other People's Money can greatly expand your production capacity.

Louis A. was a computer hobbyist who noted that a lot of small businesses were installing microcomputers to help with their bookkeeping, billing, and inventory work. Most very small computers of the type these businesses use come with a 90-day guarantee, and after that it's up to the businessman to arrange his own servicing. He can send it back to the factory, but that can leave him without a computer for weeks on end.

Lou decided to go into the business of repairing these small computers. Usually, the repairs could be accomplished "on location" but at the most he might have to take a circuit board back to his home shop for a day or two.

His business did exceptionally well—so well, in fact, that work began to back up in his shop. And a backlog of calls prevented him from responding within 24 hours, as he had been accustomed to do.

The answer? OPL, which stands for Other People's Labor. "I wasn't able to find a computer technician to help me out," Lou says, "but I did hire a former TV technician who knew enough about electronics to be able to trace the problem to a particular circuit board, and to remove and replace that board."

Lou's idea was to send his technician out on all service calls, replace the troublesome circuit board, and bring the faulty one back to the shop where Lou could repair it. This solved one problem for Lou— enabling him to provide speedy service—but it also presented a new problem.

"The new problem," he explains, "was that I had to have working circuit boards ready to install as replacements for defective units. Previously, all I'd had to do was replace individual components such as transistors, integrated circuits, or burned out capacitors. It was easy to keep these in stock, but with dozens of computer brands on the market, the new system meant I'd have to have hundreds of complete circuit boards in stock. My stock would be replenished with the units removed for repair, but I still needed a supply of boards to start with."

The answer to this second problem? OPM, which stands for Other People's Money.

"I had a going business with a proven track record, and so it was easy for me to get approval for a commercial loan at my bank. This enabled me to buy all the circuit boards I needed, plus an IC tester that I'd been wanting. Now I'm able to handle many more customer calls than before, the loan has long been repaid, and the net profit is twice what it was before I began the expansion process."

Lou's profit last year? More than $45,000, he tells me.

WHEN YOU SHOULD CONSIDER OPL AND OPM

You'll remember the advice I gave a bit earlier about starting your business on a very small scale with a minimum of equipment and a small investment. That's to provide you with a "break-in" period so that you won't make expensive mistakes that a bit more experience would have shown you how to avoid. But once your business is firmly established and you do, indeed, know the ropes, the time to think about using OPL and OPM has arrived.

Take a piece of paper and figure out the total monthly cost to you for additional labor, loan repayments, and interest. Then, based on the experience you've already had, estimate how much additional revenue can be created by the proposed expansion. If the revenue figure isn't at least 125% of the total cost, you would do well to delay expanding for the time being.

It's good to know, however, that a business built on your personal skills can be expanded beyond your own personal production capacity. After all, if Henry Ford had been limited to selling only the cars he could personally produce in his little workshop, where would the Ford Motor Company be today?

13

Twenty-One Additional Ways To Make Money In Your Spare Time

We've covered a lot of ground since the opening pages of this book—hundreds of business plans in 11 different categories. Each of the chapters has dealt with businesses having a common theme. This chapter is a bit different in that there's a broad variety of plans in many categories. As in other chapters, though, each of the businesses has outstanding potential, can be started with less than $1,500, and can be run in your spare time.

So why this chapter—a potpourri of 21 different business plans? It's here because some of the business plans you're about to learn of don't fit into any of the earlier chapter categories in this book. Or, if mentioned earlier, they could not be given the space they deserved. In this chapter we have the opportunity to discuss them in greater detail.

APARTMENT BULLETIN

In many of our larger cities there are apartment referral agencies where apartment-hunters pay $20-$50 to see a list of available apartments that match their price and size needs. But setting up such an agency requires a downtown office and it often involves dealing with a considerable amount of municipal red tape. Here's a plan that does not require the rental of office space and should greatly reduce the red tape—if, indeed, there is any at all.

Why not do as Irma Y. does and publish a semi-weekly or monthly apartment bulletin? It provides the same basic service as an apartment referral agency—listing available apartments—but clients can obtain it at less cost. What you lose in profit per client you gain in volume of sales.

Irma sells each issue for $5.00. For that money, people who buy the bulletin receive a comprehensive listing of virtually all the available apartments in and around the community it serves. The bulletin is sold on newsstands (it is sealed so that browsers don't get free peeks) and in real estate offices.

Real estate offices? "Yes," says Irma, "because, you see, many brokers don't want to get involved in apartment rentals. There isn't enough money in it for them when they can make thousands of dollars on home sales. So when people stop in looking for an apartment, they sell them my bulletin and make a quick $2 profit."

How does Irma obtain her apartment listings? First of all, all listings (which are printed in classified ad form) are inserted for free. Irma knows that if she charged, a lot of good apartments would never be included. She runs a regular ad in the Yellow Pages and in the newspaper classified section explaining how the free ads can be inserted. Many brokers who receive inquiries from landlords also refer those inquiries to Irma.

"To round it out," she reports, "I also scour the newspaper classifieds and include all of the listed apartment rentals. Many of these newspaper ads run for only three days and apartment hunters who don't happen to see them can still learn of the availabilities in my bulletin."

There are also some paid display ads that are placed by owners of large apartment buildings and by banks and other businesses seeking to reach newcomers to the area. This provides welcome additional revenue with a minimum of work.

Irma types up her listings each month and then takes the sheets to a quick print shop. Here's the cost and profit breakdown:

Cost:

Printing	$300.00
Administrative	65.00
Total Cost	365.00

Income

Net Sales	$1,500.00
Advertising	500.00
Total Revenue ...	2,000.00

Profit:

Revenue	$2,000.00
Cost	365.00
Net Profit	$1,635.00

Thus, her monthly bulletin earns about $400 a week for Irma. And the beautiful thing about it is that it is still a part-time undertaking. Irma fits her duties in and around her busy schedule as the mother of three young children. If you live in an area that has many apartment buildings and if you can fit in a few dozen hours per month, this could very well be the business for you.

BOOTH SPACE

What's better than running your own store? Having six, ten, or twenty other people run it for you! And that's precisely what happens when you create a mini-mall, renting booths to individuals who set up shop selling their wares.

Sometimes such mini-malls have a common theme. All of the booth operators may be selling antiques. Or all of them may be selling crafts-related products. But generally there is a conglomeration of shops with widely varying products of a type not usually found in department stores and discount houses.

Where can the mall be located?

- Storefront
- Barn
- Vacant house in a business district
- Converted warehouse

Getting set up can be easy and inexpensive. Here are the steps involved:

1. Find a suitable building in an easily accessible location.
2. After renting the building, mark out, at least on paper, the various booth spaces. (Don't actually partition them yet, as some merchants may want double or even triple space.)

3. Publicly announce plans for the mall through advertising and press releases. Also place ads for merchant-tenants in the "Business Opportunities" section of the newspaper classified columns.

4. After signing up tenants, provide the partitions to separate the various booths. (Or, if the mini-mall is to be in a house, the existing rooms already provide most of the partitioning you need.)

5. Prepare for the grand opening, put a sign up in front, and order advertising that is paid for jointly by the tenants.

A highly successful antique mall was opened in a Hudson Valley village several years ago, with the proprietor following the general guidelines above. It is located in a vacant store on the main street of the village and it also includes what were formerly apartments over the store. The building is rented by the operator for $300 a month, and the various booths and mini-shops bring in more than $1,500 each month in rentals.

BUSINESS CO-OP

Business firms are not always competing against each other. Sometimes they cooperate with one another, especially when they can obtain needed equipment or services at lower cost by sharing with other firms.

How can you fit in? By being the coordinator who sees that each firm gets the equipment or service when and as needed. For example, Gerry L. noticed that several furniture stores in his town each maintained their own warehouses, some of which were pretty dilapidated. Knowing an opportunity when he saw one, Gerry took out a lease on a large vacant warehouse and then offered each of the furniture stores an opportunity to buy what he called "participating shares" in the storage operation. What he's doing, in effect, is sub-leasing part of the building to each participant.

Some other business co-op possibilities include:

- After-Hours Answering Service
- Computer Timesharing
- Co-Op Advertising Circular
- Promotional Events
- Store Delivery Trucks
- WATS Phone Line (800 Exchange)

When several business firms share the cost, items such as those listed above become a lot more affordable. And your role in coordinating the project is worth money that they will gladly pay.

BUSINESS DIRECTORY

Businesses that sell to other businesses naturally need to know where those businesses are. Hence the need for business directories listing a great many firms operating in a particular field.

Name a type of business (shoe manufacturing, newsletter publishing, TV wholesaling) and there's a need for a business directory. Naturally, in most fields such directories already exist. But a number of fields are not yet covered, and if you can find one of these and come up with the listings, you've got yourself a potential money-maker.

Here's how to go about it:

1. Go to a large library and examine books on trade associations and catalog listings of trade directories until you find a field that is not covered.
2. Start compiling names of businesses in the field by noting the names and addresses of all firms which advertise in consumer or trade magazines, and by renting a mailing list and sending a form letter to each firm on the list offering a free listing in your forthcoming directory.
3. Publish your directory and then offer it for sale through the mail to the kinds of businesses that are likely to want to sell various products and services to the companies in the category you have chosen.
4. Plan to update and re-issue your directory on an annual basis.

Trade directories can sell for $35, $60, or even more. That's why it is such a highly profitable field. It takes considerable research and paperwork to get started but after your first year's issue has been published, updating and revising it for subsequent "annuals" is relatively easy, and you can build a lifetime income.

CONCESSIONAIRE

Here's a business where the location, the equipment, and the customers are all supplied to you. Usually, the only investment is in merchandise and supplies—the items you sell. And concessions are available in a wide variety of fields, matching your experience, or, in some cases, needing no experience at all.

Concessionaires generally work on a commission basis with the "host" organization supplying a park, yacht club, country club, or other group or locale with a needed service.

As a concessionaire, you may be running a food stand, a gas dock at a yacht club, the pro shop at a country club, the balloon concession in a public park, one of the rides at an amusement area, the quick-photo studio in a tourist center, the pastel portrait booth at a theme park, or any of a dozen other types of money-making operations.

You can learn about available concessions by checking the "Business Opportunities" columns of your newspaper's classified section or a trade publication in the field you are considering. Also check legal ads, because when municipalities seek concessionaires they generally are required by law to run such fine-print advertisements.

HOME RENTAL MANAGEMENT

When some people move to another section of the country they prefer not to sell their homes. They may plan on returning some day after an employment assignment in a distant city is completed. Or they may simply want to keep the home in the family without currently having anyone in their family ready to move in.

Whatever the reason, these people almost always rent out the homes—and this presents the problem of supervision. Who will see that the rent is paid on time, that the home is not allowed to deteriorate, that taxes are paid, and that new tenants are found when someone moves out? You can be that person, and earn 5% of the monthly rental.

Real estate brokers are not usually interested in these arrangements, preferring to devote their time to home sales and management of large apartment buildings. With all their overhead, they don't find single-home rentals profitable. But operated out of your own home, the arrangement can be very profitable for you. Five percent of a $350 monthly rental is $17.50. Have 20 homes on your list and this can total $350. And that's for pleasant duties that involve mostly paperwork handled in your free time.

Clients are found by placing classified ads in the real estate columns and by notifying real estate brokers of your availability.

INSTANT SANDWICHES

Opening a restaurant—even a luncheonette—can be expensive. But you can go into the fast food business and even steal a few customers from the McDonalds and Burger Kings of this world by selling fast food on location.

You've guessed the type of fast food I'm referring to. Not hamburgers but conventional sandwiches, filled with such goodies as cold cuts, salads, and cheeses. This way, you can prepare the fillings ahead of time, ready for instant application to the bread upon the receipt of each order. This enables you to rival the famous fast food outlets when it comes to speed, and that's what Americans want these days.

You can sell your instant sandwiches from a wagon you roll through business office buildings, from a truck you park at construction sites, even from a station wagon you take to factory gates as the workers are entering for the morning shift (they get box lunches to take in with them). Most other mobile fast food units are limited to hot dogs. Feature sandwiches and you should be able to outsell them at every stop.

MESSAGE SERVICE

You can make good money by taking messages for busy people. What you do is have their phone calls switched to your home phone (the phone company can arrange this through an internal switching or your clients can list your number as their own) so that you receive the calls and jot down any messages for them. They call in periodically to pick up the messages.

Why would anybody want this service (selling for $20 or more a month) when a telephone answering device can be purchased cheaply? They want it because they know many callers are "turned off" by such answering machines and will refuse to leave any message.

In a Western state, Grace M. runs just such a service from a spare bedroom of her home. She started by using one telephone, but business has become so brisk that she's added several other lines. Her net income is $1,600 a month.

MINI-MUSEUM

Your home—or a building you rent—can become a tourist attraction. Americans on vacation love to stop at unusual or unique places, and if you can provide this (and you're in a well-traveled area) you have a potential gold mine. It takes a little imagination to come up with an idea suitable for your area, but the potential is tremendous. Consider what some people are already doing:

- In New York State, a home from the colonial period has been restored and the grounds manicured. The owner and some employees dress up in colonial costume to provide guided tours—charging admission, of course.

- The owner of a Victorian mansion in the Midwest has redone the interior to resemble a haunted house, complete with ghostly sounds, apparitions, a secret staircase, and other thrills. It draws hundreds of visitors, young and old, each week.

- In the Western town where a famous gunslinger of the 1800's did most of his shooting-'em-up, a store has been converted into a museum where his life story is told through artifacts and other displays.

- A fire buff whose hobby has been collecting fire engines and other firefighting paraphernalia has put the items on display inside a barn on the property behind his home. Kids love it and drag their parents there from miles around. A significant number of the visitors are firemen themselves.

Dozens of other examples could be given, but by now you get the idea. All that remains is for you to come up with a good theme of your own. But don't forget the advice I've given several times earlier in this book: Be sure to cash in on "impulse" sales by having mementos, postcards, and perhaps even refreshments on sale. After all, if the Disney corporation makes more money from such sales than it does from admissions to its two major theme parks, why shouldn't you do the same?

MINI-BUS CHARTERS

Most bus companies don't have 12- and 15-seat mini-buses available for charter. They claim that with their union rules and other overhead costs it's not profitable—but it can be profitable for you.

You'll get loads of business if you have a mini-bus ready to take small groups on outings such as theater parties, sports events, or senior citizens' gatherings. You can't buy a mini-bus for under our investment maximum of $1,500, but you can obtain a used, fully serviceable vehicle with a down payment of that amount. Start with one bus, driving it yourself, and as business grows add other vehicles and part-time drivers.

PAPERBACK BOOK EXCHANGE

What do you do with a paperback book when you're finished reading it? If you're like most people, you toss it out and buy another one. What would you do if you could get another paperback for the "turn-in" of two books you've finished reading? If you're smart, you'd take advantage of the offer.

And so would a lot of other people. That's why the paperback book exchange operated by Betty D. is such a success. Her business is located in the enclosed front porch of her home, which is near the center of the town where she lives. The porch is lined with shelves containing the thousands of paperbacks she has available.

If it's an exchange arrangement, how does Betty make any money? From the fact that people usually end up wanting more books than they're qualified to get through "trade-ins." That means they have to put up cash.

"And quite a few people stop by with no books at all to turn in. They are cash customers," Betty explains. She charges one-half the price that's printed on the cover.

"I never have to leave home," Betty boasts. "And I don't have to deal with suppliers. Nor do I have any cash tied up in inventory, because except for my starting stock all of the books came to me as turn-ins."

Betty is not getting rich, but she can't think of an easier or more enjoyable way to earn $80-$120 a week.

PERSONALIZED GREETING CARDS

When Arthur V. bought a home computer his plan was merely to use it to learn about computers and perhaps program it to play some games. Then one Christmas season he got the idea of using it to send out personalized Christmas cards.

"Most personalized Christmas cards have the sender's name imprinted on them," he points out, "but my idea was to personalize each card with the name of the recipient printed in the shape of a Christmas tree. And if I say so myself, it was a unique idea. That first year, I bought standard cards and glued a computer printout to the blank side opposite the interior greeting. Computers—even small ones—can handle this easily. After I programmed it, all I had to do was type in the names of each of the families on my Christmas list, and the computer produced individual printouts."

To show you what it looked like, let's imagine that Art has friends named Mary and John Doe. The Christmas card they would have received from him would look like any other until they opened it up. Then, inside on the left, they would see something like this:

```
                T
               TO*
              TO*MA
             TO*MARY
            TO*MARY*A
           TO*MARY*AND
          TO*MARY*AND*J
         TO*MARY*AND*JOH
        TO*MARY*AND*JOHN*
       TO*MARY*AND*JOHN*DO
      TO*MARY*AND*JOHN*DOE*
     TO*MARY*AND*JOHN*DOE*A*
    TO*MARY*AND*JOHN*DOE*A*ME
   TO*MARY*AND*JOHN*DOE*A*MERR
  TO*MARY*AND*JOHN*DOE*A*MERRY*
 TO*MARY*AND*JOHN*DOE*A*MERRY*CH
TO*MARY*AND*JOHN*DOE*A*MERRY*CHRI
TO*MARY*AND*JOHN*DOE*A*MERRY*CHRIST
TO*MARY*AND*JOHN*DOE*A*MERRY*CHRISTMA
TO*MARY*AND*JOHN*DOE*A*MERRY*CHRISTMAS!
               !!!
```

Soon after Christmas that year, Art was struck with another idea. If his friends were impressed by the card (as they were) why couldn't businesses send something like it to their clients? With a little imagination, he could come up with a number of "personalization" picture ideas including more than just Christmas trees, and all he'd have to do is type the name of the recipient. The computer would do the rest!

Art programmed some samples into his computer and then sent them out to a number of business firms. Nearly half placed sizable orders. His list of Yuletide customers has grown each year.

It isn't hard to learn how to program a home computer to do this type of work. All Art did was buy a $10 book that is available in any computer store.

His income each Christmas season is better than $15,000. The idea is so new that there's plenty of room for others to move in.

PHOTO FUND-RAISING

If you're a good photographer and would like a camera-based business located in the best business location—without having to rent a store—this could be the plan for you. You can make money by taking children's portraits in department stores and malls.

You get permission to do this without paying steep rent by getting non-profit organizations to sponsor you. They get a percentage (20% is about right) of your proceeds. Any commercial photographer will tell you that's a lot less than he has to pay for overhead, so you'll do very well financially. The store agrees to let you in because of the fund-raising nature of the project.

No advertising is needed because all promotion is handled by the sponsoring organization—and, besides, hundreds or thousands of shoppers will be passing your location each day.

It would be hard to find a business easier to enter, cheaper to launch, or more lucrative to run than this.

PRODUCT INSTALLATION

Want to make double profits? Then go into the product installation business. This involves the dual function of selling and then installing items that the buyer cannot or does not want to install himself. When he gets you to install it, part of the arrangement is that he buys the item from you, and that's where your double profits come from.

Here are just a few of the product installation fields you can enter for less than $1,500:

Boat Canvas	Mobile Radios
Burglar Alarm Systems	Mufflers
Chain Link Fences	Paging Systems
Draperies	Rooftop Antennas
Electric Motors	Shower Stalls
Folding Doors	Skylights
Garage Door Openers	Slipcovers
Heaters	Trailer Hitches
Kitchen Cabinets	Wallpaper
Locks	Wrought Iron Railings

RENT-A-HALL

You know about people sub-leasing apartments, and you read earlier in this chapter about sub-leasing warehouse space. Now give some thought to sub-leasing meeting space.

Here's how to get into this type of business inexpensively. Rent a vacant store in a good neighborhood, install some collapsible room dividers, buy some stackable chairs, and announce the availability of meeting-room space for community organizations, business conferences, receptions, training classes, seminars, press conferences, small trade shows, lectures, and all other small- to medium-sized gatherings.

One person who has done this successfully is Alfred H. He recognized the need for such a meeting place when the company for which he worked needed some space and was unable to rent the local school auditorium because the facility was not available for commercial or religious purposes. Alfred, however, found a large vacant store nearby. He can accommodate several small gatherings at the same time, thanks to folding room dividers, and he can also accept larger gatherings of up to 125 persons.

"I pay $300 a month in rent," he reports, "and it's a rare month when I don't take in at least eight times that amount."

RESTAURANT FREEBIES

The two words you see above are the name of a business operated in a suburban county outside a major Northeastern city. The business has three functions. It provides:

• Excellent advertising for restaurants
• Big savings for restaurant patrons
• Impressive profits for its owner

The arrangement offers restaurant-goers half-price on a dinner for two at any participating restaurant. They get this privilege by paying a $10 registration fee. Then they're presented with half-price meal tickets that are redeemable at more than a dozen eateries.

"Actually, rather than advertise it as half-price, I tout it as one free dinner and one regular-priced dinner," businessman Everett S. reports. "It sounds better that way, and it goes along with the name Restaurant Freebies."

The restaurants like the plan because it gets new people into their establishments. They're gambling that most of them will return. Everett has about 1,000 patron-registrants. Since each ticket is good for only one visit to each restaurant, many of his registrants renew frequently. He's taking in more than $17,000 a year in what remains a part-time business.

SERVICE AGENCY

"Let *our* fingers do the walking for you."

That's the motto of the business run by Lucy N. and Christine H. Their job is to fulfill unusual requests from paying clients. Someone needs a Rolls Royce to take him to a reception? Someone else wants a sky-writing airplane to write a love message above his true love's home? Lucy and Christine come to the rescue. They don't do it themselves, of course. But they find out who can fill the request and they hire that person—keeping a commission for themselves.

"We won't do anything cruel," Lucy explains, "and, naturally, the request must be completely legal and honorable. Otherwise, we can arrange almost anything anybody wants."

Their business was started two years ago and is now taking in more than $70,000 a year. Lucy and Christine rarely have to leave their modest office; most of the arrangements are made over the telephone.

What does it take to tap this potential source of profit in your own town? Ingenuity, mainly. Although in many cases your fingers will indeed "do the walking" (many of the required services can be found in the Yellow Pages), quite often you'll have to do some detective work and make a number of phone calls before you connect with the right person to do the job requested by a client. As your business develops, however, you'll be building up a growing file of "service sources" to call on again and again.

SHOPPER STUFFERS

One of the biggest expenses in publishing advertising handbills is distributing them to the public. You can avoid most of that problem by publishing handbills that the advertisers distribute themselves. Here's how it works:

1. You sign up a number of merchants in town who buy advertising in your handbill.

2. After the handbill is printed, you distribute it to each of the participating merchants.

3. Each of the merchants then includes a copy of the handbill with the merchandise that he hands his customers.

This is what is known as an advertising "stuffer" because it is often stuffed into the bag or parcel of goods bought by the customer. The merchant readily cooperates in the program because he knows that, just as the stuffer he includes in his outgoing packages is advertising other stores in town, each of the customers in the other stores is presented with the same stuffer—and among the ads it includes is one touting his store.

But the main attraction of this plan is that the advertisers are reaching the people they most want to reach—the shoppers who are known to do their shopping in that particular area.

As one merchant commented, "When I advertise in the regular newspaper, I'm paying for a lot of 'waste' circulation because many of its readers never shop in this particular section. But when I use the stuffer, I'm getting my message out to the very people who have proven themselves to be local shoppers."

STEREO SERVICE

When your TV breaks down, you call in a repairman. But what do people do when a component in their stereo system goes on the blitz? If they've got expensive high quality systems, they don't want to take it to the everyday TV repair shop where the average technician knows more about picture tubes than he does about tape decks or FM tuners. And very often the problem cannot be isolated to one particular component, at least not by the owner.

These are the instances when a stereo service is needed—the kind that makes house calls the way TV repairmen do. If you know electronics and have worked in hi-fi, it's a field worth considering. For one thing, there's far less competition than in TV repair. For another, you can charge the higher rates that specialists demand.

TYPESETTING

You, a typesetter? Yes, in these days of photo offset printing the required equipment is a lot less complex than in the days when hot lead was poured out of Linotype machines. Nowadays, most job printing is set in what is called "cold type." Desktop machines with regular typewriter keyboards produce, on paper or film, the text that is to be reproduced. The machines can turn out various styles of type in many different sizes, meeting a broad variety of printing needs.

Many typesetting businesses are run from private homes. Individuals who have the typesetting equipment installed in their basements or playrooms are able to handle work assigned to them by local job printers, small publishers, and advertising agencies.

Secondhand equipment capable of producing cold type is always available. Check the classified columns in any metropolitan newspaper, particularly in the "Machinery" and "Equipment For Sale" columns. Also look under "Business Equipment." In some cases, you can buy the equipment on time. Where this is not possible, and if you don't have the required cash, you should be able to arrange bank financing.

USED CARS

I'm not suggesting that you open a used car lot on your front lawn. I am suggesting that by buying used cars one or two at a time, sprucing them up a bit, and then offering them for resale, you can make good money.

The key, of course, is to get good cars at bargain prices so that you can make a profit by selling them at their listed value. And you can get such bargains in one of two ways:

1. Buy from new car dealers who receive such cars as trade-ins.
2. Attend dealer auctions, where many trade-ins are disposed of at once.

Your best buys will be among cars that need some improvement in their appearance, such as touch-up painting or the repair of minor dents and scratches. This is work you should be able to handle easily.

One thing you don't do is advertise yourself as "Joe's Used Cars" or anything like that. Instead, once you have a car ready for "the market" you simply advertise it in the paper as thousands of other private owners do. If potential customers question you closely, you tell them the truth—that fixing up and selling cars is a sideline of yours. Most won't ask, however, since it's the car they're interested in, not you.

A significant advantage in private sales such as this is that you shouldn't have to offer any guarantee. Naturally, you give honest value and represent the car accurately; but because it's a private sale no one expects you to give a written 90-day warranty.

THE TIME TO START IS NOW

In the pages of this book you have been introduced to hundreds of inexpensive, easy-to-run businesses. Not all of them are for you, of course. Every person is different, with different skills, a different background, and even different goals.

But the careful reading of each chapter will have shown you at least several opportunities that are right down your alley. Now that you've finished reading the book, you should go back over the business plans that most suited your own needs. And then you should get started. I tell you to get started advisedly because many people just dream their goals away. For one reason or another, they fail to act.

Don't you be one of them. Follow the guidelines in this book, pick a business and then take the steps to get your money-making plan in action. You can continue to use this book as a valuable reference source, because many vital tips on business promotion and development are contained in each of the chapters, even the chapters that don't cover the particular category you have chosen.

So let these pages be your "silent partner." Refer to them often. And good fortune to you.

INDEX